6 50

Conrad's Measure of Man

CONRAD'S MEASURE OF MAN

By Paul L. Wiley

GORDIAN PRESS, INC.
NEW YORK
1966

Originally Published 1954
Reprinted 1966

Published by Gordian Press, Inc. by
Arrangement with the Regents of the University of
Wisconsin
Library of Congress Card Catalogue No. 66-19089

Printed in U.S.A. by
EDWARDS BROTHERS INC.
Ann Arbor, Michigan

CONTENTS

Conrad's Measure of Man

» Man is amazing, but he is not a masterpiece. . . . Perhaps the artist was a little mad. Eh? What do you think?

—Stein in *Lord Jim*

Chapter 1

INTRODUCTION

The Critical Groundwork

ON nearing the age of sixty, Joseph Conrad attained sufficient prestige as a novelist to be able to free himself of those doubts of his own powers and that dread of failure which had afflicted him as sorely as his own physical ailments and those of his wife. The measure of fame granted him by the public, whose approval he considered requisite to success, did not, however, embrace the whole of his published work but rested mainly on later books, like *Chance* and *Victory*, which made fairly liberal concessions to readers who expected novels to deal almost exclusively with lovers. In general opinion his name still evoked vague associations with the tropical jungle and the ship's cuddy, despite the fact that he himself had protested against being classified as an author of exotic or nautical yarns. At the present time, however, more than a quarter-century since his death in 1924, posthumous recognition, with its usual liberality, has risen in flood; and whereas Conrad during his lifetime bore comparison with minor authors like Blackmore and Clark Russell, he now shares in the esteem accorded to Henry James, André Gide, and other writers of equal renown.

The only matter for surprise in this widespread acknowledgment of Conrad's importance is its long delay. The passage of time has done very little to dull the vitality of his books, as it has with some of those of such earlier British novelists as Galsworthy, Bennett, and Wells; and even though changes in popular taste and critical judgment have caused preference to shift from one part of his writing to another, the admirer of Conrad, like the modern devotee of Herman Melville, can undertake a thorough study of all of his work with the certainty of profit and with no serious loss in interest or enjoyment. As strong, likewise, as his appeal to the common reader has been his influence upon other writers. In various ways authors so well known as Ford Madox Ford, Santayana, T. S. Eliot, Scott Fitzgerald, Ernest Hemingway, and Graham Greene—to mention only a few familiar names—have either learned from him or have responded to the force of his style and vision. Because his reputation stands secure, it is, therefore, no longer necessary to compose tributes to his achievement. The task remaining is that of a deeper comprehension of the exact nature of this achievement and of all the values that it has to yield.

Readers and critics have still to reckon with the fact that Conrad died apparently certain that no one had really come to grips with his intentions. As late as 1917 he complained to Sir Sidney Colvin that after twenty-two years of work he had not been very well understood; [1] and this statement

1. G. Jean-Aubry, *Joseph Conrad: Life and Letters*, II, 185.

would seem to indicate that his famous credo, "Before all, to make you *see*," had been interpreted rather too narrowly or literally by those who were content not to see very much beyond the brilliant strokes of visual detail on the luxuriant surfaces of his tales. Perhaps, in private, Conrad obtained satisfaction from the thought that the inner mysteries of his art remained inviolate; but in his letters he often spoke as though dismayed at failures to appreciate his more obvious aims. It was not his habit, however, to take pains to make his ideas clear to those who could not grasp them for themselves. In his correspondence with friends, like Edward Garnett, for example, he did not, as a rule, neglect the forms of courtesy in order to argue in a stubborn fashion over judgments with which he disagreed. A polite objection, a hint at the truth, a raising of the hands; and then, without having given ground in the controversy, he was ready to drop the matter. But he took differences of opinion seriously; and as he grew older and more troubled about popularity, critical mistakes made him irritable. Seeming to care less about being understood, he tightened his defense against misunderstanding. In 1922, in one of the most illuminating discussions of his art that he ever wrote, he sharply reproved his early critic, Richard Curle, for an article in which the latter had been too explicit in revealing facts about the background of some of the stories and too hasty in describing Conrad's work as gloomy or tragic. He ended the letter by snapping at his gentle disciple for calling him a "tragedian." [2]

The reprimand hurt Curle, who had meant well; but it was just, for the reader who attentively examines Conrad's

2. *Letters of Joseph Conrad to Richard Curle*, Letter No. 89.

fiction as a whole will conclude that the author was as little a tragedian as he was a comedian. Stories like *Lord Jim* and "The End of the Tether" follow a tragic pattern; but a great many of the other tales—*Typhoon*, "Falk," *Chance*—produce instead a comic or ironical effect. The same difficulty of generalized classification holds for the description of Conrad as a writer of romances or a believer in the virtues of romantic adventure. Obviously *The Secret Agent* and *Under Western Eyes* are not romantic novels. Neither are *An Outcast of the Islands*, *Nostromo*, and *Victory*, despite their superficial atmosphere of adventure in far countries. Where Conrad does introduce romantic elements, these are treated in a special manner which has no bearing upon the exotic features of his work that he did not care to have emphasized. Although broad labels of this kind may be misleading, since they suggest that his ability was confined to a single range of expression, a main fault to be found with them is that they offer little help to the reader once he has discovered all of the levels of meaning in the rich substance of Conrad's books. From his steady growth in public favor in recent years it is evident that there is a quality in his vision of life which continues to excite the modern mind; and any attempt to define this source of interest leads quickly to critical impatience with stock generalities and to a desire for the closest acquaintance with the work itself.

The critic who now undertakes a fresh evaluation of Conrad's art has at his disposal a body of fact and theory handed down by earlier workers. For a knowledge of Conrad's career through its varied phases from youth to seafaring to professional literary activity, he can turn with gratitude to the full biographical studies of G. Jean-Aubry and the more specialized researches of Gustav Morf, who concentrated upon the Polish strain in Conrad's character and possible Slavic elements in his fiction, and of John D. Gordan, who published a valuable and partly biographical account of Conrad's first stage of authorship. The results obtained by these scholars form a solid point of departure for studies of Conrad's work in every aspect.

Criticism devoted to literary rather than bibliographical matters has moved on from the general to the particular. In view of the present acceptance of Conrad as a major writer, further effort to encourage public appreciation of his talent no longer seems so necessary as it did during his lifetime or shortly after his death. This duty was creditably performed by critics like Richard Curle and Ernst Bendz and somewhat later by R. L. Mégroz. In books that surveyed his work in the broad outline suited to the general and possibly uninitiated reader, they presented essential information about his life and personality, his beliefs, his characters, his plots, and his style. Since their purpose was wide in scope, they did not explore any of these topics in a minute way; nor—with the exception of Mégroz—did they venture far into speculation on the deeper-lying motives in his writing.

In the highly important special field of Conrad's literary methods and techniques Ford Madox Ford and Edward Crankshaw, both vigorous writers, have contributed enlightening ideas. As Conrad's collaborator in several books Ford possessed firsthand knowledge of the impressionistic devices that they cultivated; and Crankshaw, in a longer and more analytical study than that of Ford, explained the complicated mechanics of a number of the stories. Although these critics were among the first to describe some of the principles by which Conrad worked, they have not exhausted the subject of his method; and they have left others to examine, in particular, the larger structural aspects of his objective manner of presentation. On the basis of what appears rather meager evidence, Ford and Crankshaw both proceeded, furthermore, on the assumption that Conrad was a brilliant craftsman with a relatively simple view of experience; and by weighing the balance so heavily on the side of technique, they tended, perhaps unintentionally, to subscribe to the opinion that he is interesting chiefly from that point of view. This theory will not bear scrutiny, for in the work of Conrad, as in that of any major novelist, method and thought are equally subtle.

In their summing up of what has been called, in the layman's sense of the term, Conrad's philosophy, Ford and Crankshaw arrived at somewhat similar conclusions. On the authority of a well-known statement by the novelist himself, Ford claimed that the notion of fidelity to an idea or a service formed the essence of Conrad's belief; [3] and Crankshaw asserted that "much of Conrad's writing may be seen as a fantasia on fidelity." [4] Other students who have dealt with this problem offer different solutions. In 1933, W. W. Bancroft devoted to this branch of the critical enterprise a complete thesis in which, using characters from the stories to

3. Ford Madox Ford, *Joseph Conrad: A Personal Remembrance*, p. 66.

4. Edward Crankshaw, *Joseph Conrad: Some Aspects of the Art of the Novel*, p. 19.

support his argument, he contended that the ideas of human solidarity and moral law were the key to Conrad's philosophical thinking.[5] Less metaphysically inclined than Bancroft, Ernst Bendz held that Conrad placed the highest value upon responsibility.[6] In addition to these statements concerning the virtues that Conrad admired, a good many philosophical epithets have been applied to him—such as idealist, nihilist, or even "pantagrist"—and only Mr. E. M. Forster seems to have been bold enough to pronounce him elusive, misty, and creedless.[7]

Since Conrad, as he himself declared to Barrett H. Clark, was a man of formed character and of certain immovably fixed conclusions when he adopted the profession of letters,[8] it is reasonable to suppose that traces of a personal philosophy can be found in his work. Quite possibly, as Crankshaw affirms, his creed was a simple one if based upon respect for such broadly human ideals as fidelity or responsibility.[9] The faith to which an artist pledges himself consciously may, however, be a thing apart from the imaginative apprehension of life that stimulates him to creative effort; and although many of Conrad's characters do exhibit traits of the worthiest kind, it does not follow necessarily that a demonstration of the value of one or another of these qualities was central to his aims. Conrad, it is evident, was not a philosophical novelist

5. William Wallace Bancroft, *Joseph Conrad: His Philosophy of Life*, *passim*. This is the main conclusion to Bancroft's argument.
6. Ernst Bendz, *Joseph Conrad: An Appreciation*, p. 91.
7. E. M. Forster, "Joseph Conrad: A Note," *Abinger Harvest*, p. 138.
8. Aubry, *Conrad: Life and Letters*, II, 204.
9. Crankshaw, *Conrad: Some Aspects*, p. 27.

in the manner of Meredith, Huxley, or Mauriac; nor was he a didactic one, though he moralized constantly and often to good purpose. His stories make so little place for abstraction or discussion of ideas that to approach them by the philosophical route seems to lead one aside from larger discoveries of another order. What the reader does find in Conrad, not in occasional passages but in the entire fabric of each of his books, is something more extensive than a personal philosophy, a profound insight into the nature of man in his relation to the world and to society.

The studies of Conrad according to the foregoing patterns—the biographical, the appreciative, the technical, the philosophical—have opened the way to a variety of attempts at revaluation, inspired to some extent by his increasing fame and carried forward in recent years by critics like Morton D. Zabel, M. C. Bradbrook, Albert Guerard, Walter F. Wright, F. R. Leavis, Douglas Hewitt, and others. The activity of these scholars, often markedly attentive to Conrad's text, has been illuminating with respect to the literary qualities of his work, the relative merits of his books, and the nature of his intellectual and moral perceptions. By the exercise of mature judgment these writers have shown that there are ranges of complexity in his writing hardly touched on by previous students; and it is apparent that criticism has reached the intensive stage inevitable for an author who so abundantly rewards investigation of this sort.

The study which follows in this book invites the reader to examine Conrad's work from a standpoint not hitherto adopted with any persistence and attempts to suggest that this manner of approach leads to an understanding of Conrad's way of viewing the role of man in the spectacle of the universe and hence of his position as an artist. In one of his letters to his friend and fellow author, Cunninghame Graham, Conrad remarked: "I don't start with an abstract notion. I start with definite images . . ."; [10] and this study begins with a consideration of recurrent strains of imagery in his stories from first to last and of concrete thematic figures, those named in the headings of the three main sections of the book, which relate closely to the images in question. The employment of materials of this kind connects directly with the general subject of Conrad's literary method; and this portion of the argument receives special attention early in Chapter II as a necessary preliminary to the later discussion of separate works. Since it is difficult, furthermore, to appreciate the significance of these themes and images without reference to some of the currents of thought and literary fashion in Conrad's time, a topic which has so far been comparatively neglected by critics, the study makes note of such relationships whenever they seem relevant to the argument. A main value of this approach should become evident in the fact that it reveals a principle of continuity in the development of Conrad's art that deserves emphasis since it corresponds to a definable vision of life which governs all phases of his work.[11]

10. Aubry, *Conrad: Life and Letters,* I, 268.

11. All references to Conrad's works, except for his letters and his dramatic version of *The Secret Agent,* are to the twenty-six–volume Kent Edition (Garden City, N. Y.: Doubleday, Page and Co., 1926). Whenever a source is readily identifiable, volume and page numbers of this edition have been inserted within parentheses in the text. Further identification is available by checking the number of the volume against the entry for Conrad's complete works in the bibliog-

The comments on method which figure prominently in the discussion pay due heed to the findings by Ford and Crankshaw that Conrad strove for what may be called, rather awkwardly, "visual" effects that appeal constantly to the eye of the reader in the effort to make him literally "see." Criticism has not, however, gone far beyond the assumption that the results of the visual technique ended in concrete and unusual renderings of scene and character, light and perspective, features which are impressive but which pertain to style in its narrowest meaning. This line of inquiry might well be extended so as to include the possibility that Conrad made use of an objective method for an even more ambitious aim: that, namely, of finding visual or dramatic equivalents for states of inner experience or for ideas embodied in his tales. Crankshaw points out, for example, that after his first two novels Conrad abandoned internal psychological analysis for the purpose of building up character; and the critic goes on to suggest that Conrad resorted in future to objective description because he was not naturally gifted with the psychological ability of some of his contemporaries.[12] At no point in his career, however, does Conrad exhibit any deficiency in psychological penetration; and his abandonment of the internal for the objective method of treatment may well have resulted from conscious preference rather than from compulsion. A recent critic, enlarging upon the fact that Conrad as well as Ford Madox Ford was adapting French practices to the English novel, refers to similarities between

---

raphy. The volume number of the Kent Edition precedes the title in notes.

12. Crankshaw, *Conrad: Some Aspects*, pp. 83, 84–85.

their theories of composition and those of the imagist poets, who also aimed at visual means of appeal; [13] and in view of this experimental tendency in his work it may be found that Conrad did not hesitate to bring psychological issues within the scope of his method.

This study seeks to establish proof that Conrad did so rely upon visual procedures that he attempted to project even the most subtle moral and psychological matters through dramatic and concrete situations. Reasons are also given for the opinion that much of his difficulty with highly troublesome novels like *The Rescue* and with other stories that have sometimes been disparaged for their retarded movement and excessive detail can be explained by the effort required to erect top-heavy visual machinery. Working along these lines, Conrad became accustomed to developing allegorical scenes or relationships between characters in order to convey the basic truths contained in his work; and it will be shown that, although this practice can be discerned in his earliest books, it is particularly evident in later novels like *Chance* and *Victory* where the concluding allegory is plotted with minute fidelity to each component in the pattern of meaning. In Chapter II it will be indicated that Conrad derived hints for the use of a method of this kind through his reading of Flaubert, a writer whose influence upon him nearly all critics have admitted without determining the positive nature of the debt, and especially through his acquaintance with *La Tentation de Saint Antoine*, an allegorical work which impressed itself upon his imagination.

Conrad's knowledge of Flaubert is merely one indication

13. Hugh Kenner, *The Poetry of Ezra Pound*, pp. 266, 268.

of the broader relationship between his art and the literary and intellectual background of the 1890's and the earlier years of the present century, the period to which the bulk of his writing belongs. Since he was alert to the temper of the age, a closer study than is possible here of this aspect of his work might well bring light to bear upon the traces in his fiction of the contemporary interest in Schopenhauer, Nietzsche, Wagner, in socialism and feminism, in religious and scientific controversy. The spread of naturalistic theory, literary or scientific, colors his writing to some degree, notably in the conception of character. In common with Zola and Maupassant, Conrad dealt with the popular naturalistic theme of individual failure, due either to circumstance or to inner weakness, and at times with abnormal states of mind, as in tales like "The Idiots," *The Secret Agent*, and *The Rover*. Many of his psychological perceptions—of the division of personality, of the conquest of mind and will by the irrational, of the maladies that inhibit action—are in close accord with the tendencies of mental science in his time, whether manifested in literature or in the case books of men like Charcot, Janet, Prince, and James.[14] Even though Conrad's drawing of character has been praised often enough, it has not, perhaps, been made sufficiently clear that with people like Lord Jim, Charles Gould, Flora de Barral, Axel Heyst he revealed insights into peculiarities of modern temperament that seem beyond the powers of most of his contemporaries in the English novel with the exception of Henry James. More important, however, to the immediate

14. See Ralph Tymms, *Doubles in Literary Psychology*, pp. 93–94.

purposes of this study than passing reference to matters like the foregoing is the evidence that the subject as well as the design of many of Conrad's stories reflects the mood of transition and intellectual conflict around the turn of the century. Opposed in this period are the older romantic and the newer realistic conceptions of character and conduct, the traditional moral values of Christianity and the naturalistic acceptance of motives of instinct and self-preservation. Such an atmosphere fosters the growth of an ironical spirit in literature; and just as earlier the work of Flaubert and later that of Anatole France, both novelists well known to Conrad, abound in the irony of contrast, so also does Conrad's writing often originate in a perception of incongruities resulting from the crisis of thought in his age and exhibiting themselves in ironic situation. Many of Conrad's finest effects are the product of the ironical vision which is one of his most distinguishing characteristics as an artist.

Conrad's irony relates to a particular view of man in a natural or a social setting; and one of the leading clues to this attitude lies in the imagery of the stories. As the reader becomes familiar with these works, the images that he is likely to remember most vividly are those which can be described as cosmic or creational within Biblical definition. The background in many of the finest tales is given depth by metaphors of order and chaos, world destruction and rebirth, Last Judgment and Deluge. A favorite scene is that of a small sphere of human endeavor—a trading station, a ship, a state, or an island—threatened by fire or flood or by the engulfment of a surrounding wilderness. With reference to character, the images of greatest frequency are those of

Fall or expulsion from Eden. They emerge when an individual who is blinded by some illusion of security or superiority descends suddenly from this paradisal state through a revelation of evil, often depicted concretely as a rank jungle to contrast with the shattered dream of order. Imagery of this kind fills so large a place in Conrad's writing that it attains almost the proportions of myth, and it is a feature which distinguishes him from the strictly realistic novelists of his time.

By placing man or the world created by him in the midst of such perilous surroundings, Conrad expressed symbolically his denial of complacent trust in human power or in human institutions. In this light his imagery of cataclysm and deterioration looks at times like a counter-myth to the ideas of individualism and progress fostered by nineteenth-century thinking and resembles to that extent the different and more elaborate mythology of Yeats, created in part out of the latter's distaste for the democratic and scientific bias of the age. As readers of his letters will recognize, Conrad, like Yeats, had in his nature a fund of aristocratic disdain for bourgeois principles. Middle-class businessmen and commercial adventurers do not fare happily in his stories, particularly the early ones; and money as a corrupting agent plays a significant role in his work from first to last. His outlook has, therefore, something in common with that of such anti-bourgeois writers in France as Flaubert, Baudelaire, and Huysmans. Like Baudelaire, for example, whose poetry he knew, Conrad had a thorough comprehension of the dualism of good and evil in man; and in many of his tales men fall by reason of original sin. Yet, essentially, his view of experience was too ample to stop short at ridicule of prevailing social beliefs; and although, as will be shown in Chapter II, he took over from French literature the hermit figure which had been used as a symbol of withdrawal from common life, he made this figure serve a much more comprehensive satirical purpose of his own. That purpose, which conforms at so many points with the humanistic thought of the Western world, is concerned with a portrayal of man as a limited human being.

In a letter of 1892 to his aunt, Mme. Poradowska, a woman to whom he laid bare his heart rather insistently, Conrad, at the age of thirty-five, stated expressly his opinion of the individual and his worth:

> The fact is, however, that one becomes useful only on realizing the utter insignificance of the individual in the scheme of the universe. When one well understands that in oneself one is nothing and that a man is worth neither more nor less than the work he accomplishes with honesty of purpose and means, and within the strict limits of his duty towards society, only then is one the master of his conscience, with the right to call himself a man. Otherwise, were he more attractive than Prince Charming, richer than Midas, wiser than Doctor Faust himself, the two-legged featherless creature is only a despicable thing sunk in the mud of all the passions. I would spoil a great deal of paper on this theme, but you doubtless understand me as well as I do myself, without further explanation.[15]

The paper that Conrad refused to spoil in an expansion of this theme for his correspondent he afterwards covered, as a man of letters, with constant observations on the dreams and follies of the two-legged featherless creature. In his essay on

15. *Letters of Joseph Conrad to Marguerite Poradowska, 1890–1920*, pp. 45–46.

Anatole France (1904) he remarked on the "irremediable littleness" of man and on the fact that France's penguins, on being turned into human beings, received the curse of original sin and all of "the labours, the miseries, the passions, and the weaknesses attached to the fallen condition of humanity." [16] In Conrad's own stories evidence by means of character goes to show that by himself the individual has no safeguard against mischance or irrational motive, and the characters who suffer most are those with the loftiest opinions of their own capacities. It is difficult, therefore, to regard Conrad as an admirer of romantic behavior. A study, for example, of the man whom Ford Madox Ford described as Conrad's most typical hero,[17] the Captain Lingard of *An Outcast of the Islands* and *The Rescue*, reveals a character bedecked rather obviously with an adventurer's romantic glamor. But the crux in these novels is Lingard's loss of authority through self-betrayal, so that he is left powerless in the end. Conrad himself called Lingard "episodically foolish," [18] and nowhere does his writing express confidence in this type of romantic adventurer and planner of utopias. Examined closely, moreover, much of Conrad's romantic paraphernalia of armed brigs and tropical intrigue in an atmosphere of celestial uproar appears overcast by irony at the expense of man's attempt to assume the attributes of Divinity.

Conrad's scepticism with regard to the divinity of man does not seem, however, to have been the outcome of any

16. Joseph Conrad, "Anatole France," III: *Notes on Life and Letters*, 33, 44.

17. Ford, *Conrad: A Personal Remembrance*, p. 167.

18. *Letters from Joseph Conrad: 1895–1924*, p. 55.

great measure of trust in Divinity itself. There are suggestions at times that he felt a certain resentment against a Providence that had abandoned mankind and the world to a fallen state. Just as his stories often contrast an imagery of divine judgment with that of a wilderness of brute struggle, so also do his letters contain reflections now on the possibility of a Creator, now on the purely mechanical nature of the universe. He could allow for the existence of a God and also speak of "the precious mess he has made of his only job." [19] Perhaps in order to assert the injustice of the cosmic scheme, Conrad endowed some of his fallen men with attributes not unworthy of a benevolent Creator. In violating the principle of limitation, these characters meet defeat; but many of them—Lord Jim, Captain Whalley, Charles Gould—are intrinsically fine and honorable. Their downfall may reflect in some degree upon the failure of their Creator to regulate the universe in his own interests.

It is not unjustifiable to suppose that there lingered in Conrad's thought a trace of regret for the replacement of a man-centered design of creation with one in which the individual and his values become insignificant. One of the impressions that Conrad retained from his seaman's life and that he employed in a memorable way in *The Nigger of the Narcissus* was that of a ship, an ordered world, moving at the center of the circle of sea and sky. In 1893 he wrote to Mme. Poradowska:

> . . . my vision is circumscribed by the sombre circle where the blue of the sea and the blue of heaven touch without merging. Moving in that perfect Circle inscribed by the Creator's hand,

19. Aubry, *Conrad: Life and Letters,* I, 213.

and of which I am always the center, I follow the undulant line of the swell. . . .[20]

Conrad's characters seldom, however, have this feeling of serenity and of place. Many of them are caught in a division between their moral, and oftentimes Christian, intentions and forms of behavior motivated by instinct, passion, unreason; and this rift within them is characteristic of an age already strained by a waning of Christian morality and the rise of creeds of irrationality and negation. In the opposing terms of this conflict, Conrad found materials essential to his art. It is often his practice to set virtues closely associated with a Christian tradition, like those of asceticism and chivalry, beside impulses of sensuality and vanity; and although the resulting incongruity often serves an ironic aim in ridiculing the mere pretense of ascetic or chivalric action as a departure from the norm of conduct, the emphasis also falls upon the decline of these ideals as determinants of behavior. In parts of his work, and especially those wherein he deals with loss of the will to live, he seems to betray apprehension that this split between systems of belief may affect the survival of Western man.

In order to illustrate as fully and concretely as possible the main factors in the argument, this study follows the procedure of commenting on a number of Conrad's principal works in the order of their composition. This method, which allows evidence to accumulate gradually, not only permits criticism to start from within the works themselves but also enables the reader to see how Conrad's treatment of leading

20. Conrad, *Letters to Poradowska*, p. 52.

images and themes accompanied his development as an artist. The analysis of individual novels and stories confines itself to larger details of structural outline so as to keep the central line of the discussion clear, and the requirement of emphasis makes it necessary to pass over many features of situation or character-portrayal that might be examined in a lengthier study. The richness of Conrad's material is everywhere presupposed, however; and it is hoped that the commentary here may help to direct attention to a few additional sources of value. For the convenience of the reader and for an easier handling of a substantial body of material, the study breaks into three main sections, each corresponding in a general way to a stage in Conrad's literary career. Although Conrad himself did not object to a division of his work and even made statements in his prefaces to indicate that he thought habitually of his writing as falling into a group order,[21] the reader is not asked to assume that the plan adopted here corresponds to any definite theory of arrangement on Conrad's part or to lay undue weight on the repeated use of terms such as "period" and "phase." The grouping does show, however, that at certain points in his career Conrad moved into new fields in order to extend the range of his subject matter and that at these times the nature of his inspiration underwent a decided change.

The close bearing of the argument upon the examples of Conrad's writing brought forward for reference may also induce the reader to test this approach by turning to the works themselves, particularly those that have been some-

21. Conrad, XVI: *Youth: A Narrative, and Two Other Stories*, ix; XIII: *The Secret Agent*, viii–ix.

what neglected by critical appraisal. Although scholars have disagreed with respect to the finer points of merit in Conrad's art, fairly general consent as to his most successful and readable books seems to have been reached. To reckon up his failures (for like other writers he must be allotted his share) is a more hazardous task. In this study attention singles out certain works that have usually been dispraised—stories like "The Return," "The Informer," "The Planter of Malata"—and others that have often been called inferior—earlier novels like *Almayer's Folly* and *An Outcast of the Islands* and later ones like *The Arrow of Gold*, *The Rover*, and perhaps *The Rescue*. With respect to the inferiority of the novels last named, this opinion appears to rest upon a slighter estimation of their content and aim than this study would admit; and the argument attempts to make clear what Conrad intended in these books. The Malayan novels, though slow in pace, offer so many insights into his major themes that it is a mistake to dismiss them as sallies into the exotic. The later novels suffer from technical strain, but they are interesting not only because they develop a new aspect of his art in its final phase but also because they furnish proof that he was experimenting up to the end of his life. The stories mentioned are less noteworthy as separate pieces than they are as links in his expanding design. It is possible that he tried out in some of these shorter tales the material used in longer and better-finished stories. Thus "The Return" appears the forerunner to a novel of metropolitan life, "The Informer" anticipates in many ways *The Secret Agent*, and "The Planter of Malata" looks forward to *The Arrow of Gold* and *The Rescue*. A further aid to the reader who wishes to rank Conrad's books may be found in the writer's own Author's Notes. Unlike numerous other artists Conrad was a fairly sound judge of his own accomplishment, and his comments on his best and weakest efforts are always incisive.

Chapter 2

THE HERMIT

Man in the World

THOUGH a master of the art of words, Conrad also became adept in the exploration of mental states, among which he considered the morbid a legitimate subject for the novelist.[1] John Gordan has noted the theme of human disintegration in Conrad's earliest books; [2] and if the body of fiction from *Almayer's Folly* through the *Typhoon* volume may be taken to form a period, every story in this group touches on a psychological problem which results, or threatens to result, in human failure.

During this period, moreover, Conrad was struggling with technical procedures of unusual difficulty which sharpened his vexation over the delayed progress of *The Rescue*, under way in 1896 but not completed until 1919. Cursing the work in his letters to Edward Garnett, he declared that his very

1. G. Jean-Aubry, *Joseph Conrad: Life and Letters*, II, 78.
2. John D. Gordan, *Joseph Conrad: The Making of a Novelist*, p. 28.

being seemed "faded and thin like the ghost of a blonde and sentimental woman, haunting romantic ruins pervaded by rats." [3] From these cries of distress part of his trouble with the novel appears to have been caused by his endeavor to apply a method of visual presentation to psychological material,[4] and evidence from other work at this stage of his career supports this point of view. Writing, for example, in defense of his story, "The Return" (1898), to Garnett, who thought it poor as most subsequent critics have done, Conrad said of the principal character, Alvan Hervey, "I wanted the reader to *see him think*. . . ." [5] Since Conrad promised to be grateful for any kind word about this tale that cost him so much "in toil, temper, and disillusion," [6] a brief light on its content and technique may show that it holds an important place in his development.

In its metropolitan setting and in narrative method, no other story by the early Conrad is quite like "The Return." Yet readers of the Malayan tales will find the theme familiar. It concerns a wealthy businessman—a silk-hatted double for the egotistical Willems of *An Outcast of the Islands*—who, having married for vanity rather than love, finds his assurance wrecked by his wife's infidelity. When passion ignored breaks Hervey's reserve, he sees around him, as if by a lightning flash, a jungle landscape wherein he stands fearful, lonely, and betrayed. This revelation of evil compels him to recognize that he is compromised between his principles of

3. *Letters from Joseph Conrad: 1895–1924*, p. 59.
4. *Ibid.*, p. 141.
5. *Ibid.*, p. 107.
6. Conrad, in VIII: *Tales of Unrest*, xi.

self-restraint on the one hand and sexual instinct on the other; and to avoid this dilemma, he abandons the house and the woman to find salvation in a world of toil.

Although the reader is not altogether sure whether the wife has triumphed in her contempt for Hervey's bourgeois ideals or whether the husband gains in the end through moral understanding, the irony at Hervey's expense is unequivocal; and it is conveyed in part through an ingenious handling of atmosphere. Hervey thinks himself a high priest in the "temple" of his house (VIII, 155–56), but he is really a sham ascetic with his hollow creed and blind subjection to desire. As the full prospect of his depravity opens before him, the house—by a process that Conrad called "sublimated description" (VIII, x)—turns by stages from a Victorian town residence with a quantity of plush, brass, and slightly obscene statuary into a tomb, an inferno, and a genteel brothel (VIII, 184)—a temple profaned and sinking under the rising shadow of a deluge (VIII, 182).

Despite this remarkable background imagery "The Return" is not completely effective. The action lags under a disclosure of Hervey's thoughts in a state of anguish which seems unduly prolonged and rather unconvincing, not because the analysis is faulty but because it is excessive for a nature as coarse as that of Hervey. But together with analysis Conrad also attempted, as he explained to Garnett, to make the reader "see Hervey think" by introducing a series of visual images—erupting volcanoes, earthquakes, floods of lava—which not only give a strained impression of the explosive quality of mental shock but also clog the narrative. This mingling of analysis and visual detail resulted in a ponderous style which hampered a free display of Conrad's talents. But as evidence of his interest in visualizing psychological data, the story is instructive.

Besides the method itself the predicament of the central character also commands attention. Conrad, the reader will remember, compares Hervey to a mock priest in a cloistered house with a smug belief in his chastity according to the conventions of his class. His vision of a wilderness startles him out of his complacency and excludes him from his false Eden:

> He was a simple human being removed from the delightful world of crescents and squares. He stood alone, naked and afraid, like the first man on the first day of evil. There are in life events, contacts, glimpses, that seem brutally to bring all the past to a close. There is a shock and a crash, as of a gate flung to behind one by the perfidious hand of fate. Go and seek another paradise, fool or sage.
>
> (VIII, 134)

The man's discovery of his isolated condition in a fallen world marks an essential resemblance between "The Return" and the rest of Conrad's early work. The wilderness revealed to Hervey becomes a unifying symbol, an image that reappears under different forms from the tropical forest of *Almayer's Folly* to Hagberd's weedy garden in "To-Morrow" and that occurs in Conrad's later writing as well.

The meaning of this image is not fixed, although its character is more precise in *Almayer's Folly* and *An Outcast of the Islands* where it appears as nature in erotic guise. But of main importance is the fact that it regularly symbolizes a state of removal from the theater of normal and collective life, often represented by that of the open sea, and thus a field for abnormal experience. Hervey is a prototype of the lonely figure in this landscape; for like him, all of Conrad's other prisoners of the wilderness are solitaries—hermits divided between mind and will, virtue and vice, morality and instinct—and frequently visionaries subject to either paradisal or infernal hallucinations.

The prominence given to these figures tormented in solitude calls attention to Conrad's familiarity with French literature of the nineteenth century, especially that current wherein Flaubert and Baudelaire proved formative influences. Although the full extent of Conrad's reading in French is not certainly known, the proof that it was wide can be gathered from his own statements, his literary essays, and a variety of quotations and allusions in his work.[7] His knowledge, in particular, of Flaubert, among others of "les mauvais maitres" whom he had studied, antedated the completion of his first book, *Almayer's Folly*, as may be seen from a letter in praise of *Madame Bovary* that he wrote to Mme. Poradowska in 1892.[8] In a letter of special interest, to Hugh Walpole in 1918, Conrad remarked that Flaubert's *La Tentation de Saint-Antoine* and *L'Education sentimentale* were the books that he cared most about and these "only from the point of view of the rendering of concrete things and visual impressions." [9] If, as he says, he learned nothing from Flaubert, the French novelist did rouse in him a spirit of emu-

7. See G. Jean-Aubry, *Vie de Conrad*, pp. 198–99.
8. *Letters of Joseph Conrad to Marguerite Poradowska, 1890–1920*, p. 44.
9. Aubry, *Conrad: Life and Letters*, II, 206.

lation; and it is reasonable to assume that the portrayal of the solitary and his temptations in the *Saint-Antoine* gave Conrad, if not a model, at least a remarkable likeness to the hermit type which occupied his imagination to the end of his career. In his essay on Maupassant (1904) he recalled specifically "the glittering cortege of deadly sins passing before the austere anchorite in the desert air of Thebaïde." [10] Even his last and unfinished novel, *Suspense* (1925), contains a hermit in the wilderness.

One need not, however, rely on the *Saint-Antoine* alone for proof that the solitary drawn by Conrad was a type well established in the literary tradition of the period. For Baudelaire the solitude of the dandy absorbed in his horror of mediocrity was a kind of Thebaïd; [11] and the Des Esseintes in Huysmans' *A Rebours* dreamt of a desert hermitage, combined with modern comfort, "a refined Thebaïd," where he could fly for refuge from human folly.[12] For these French writers, therefore, the hermit Saint Anthony, a familiar subject in literature and painting from past to present, became associated with their own contempt for the common life of their day or symbolized, as with Flaubert, the retreat of the artist into his own separate realm.[13] Flaubert's anchorite seems, in fact, to have been but the most complete literary projection of a quality of temperament peculiar not only to Flaubert himself but also to other souls confined, in their disdain for the ordinary, to an isolation wherein traditional

10. Conrad, III: *Notes on Life and Letters*, 26–27.
11. André Ferran, *L'Esthétique de Baudelaire*, p. 65.
12. J.-K. Huysmans, *Against the Grain*, p. 82.
13. See A. Baillot, *Influence de la philosophie de Schopenhauer en France (1860–1900)*, p. 214.

religious and moral ideas became inverted or confused in the quest for aesthetic delights or for a way to paradise through the senses. Isolation led, moreover, to discoveries of a psychological kind with reference to man's capacities for heaven and hell which Baudelaire made by a descent into the darkness within himself and Des Esseintes by a home course in forbidden pleasures. Like Flaubert's saint the modern solitary found that his escape from the mundane involved a private encounter with demons who swarmed upon him in his cell in the wilderness. The hermit at the same time ascetic and sensual stands, therefore, not only as a creature of what has been called the decadent imagination but also as a representative of a complex psychological condition. He enlarges the range of character study in literature.

Conrad's own treatment of the hermit figure is distinctive in the ironical cast of his attitude and in his placing of emphasis on the tension between the solitary in his withdrawal and a community threatened by a failure of moral bonds. But the elaborate records of states of crisis in the isolated individual in stories like *An Outcast*, *Lord Jim*, and *Typhoon* leave little doubt that Conrad's psychological assumptions accorded closely with the thought of his time, especially as represented by those French writers already mentioned. Even as Flaubert and Baudelaire had known and analyzed the strife of idealism and sensuality, the paralysis of will, and the nihilism of the ailing modern soul, so also Conrad occupied himself with these and other symptoms of what the scientific jargon of the period often named vaguely hysteria and the popular critical vocabulary, in a more ominous fashion, *mal du siècle*. Like his contemporaries he treats the enfeeblement of will as a major cause of failure; and in many incidents of great force in his earlier work the mind, operating independently of other vital functions, remains clear yet powerless to check the corruption of the will possessed, as though satanically, by passions, among which fear is the most stubborn. French authors recognized fear as a part of "the malady of the decadence," but in modern British fiction Conrad is eminent in tracing the swift deterioration of the human being gripped by terror.[14]

Many of Conrad's letters—like the bitter one addressed to Cunninghame Graham on January 31, 1898 [15]—show that he regarded sadly the isolation of the mind in a world devoid of human values where the irrational imperils reason. The melancholy of his early tales likewise reflects this mood. These stories, written shortly before and after the turn of the century when theories of the decline of Western civilization circulated freely, retain a peculiar significance because they express so vigorous an awareness that the severance of conscious mind from the unconscious powers that it should control leads to a dissolution of the bond between men in a community, that "solidarity of mankind" in which Conrad believed.[16] Nearly all of the failures which he depicts suffer in one way or another from the ailment of inner division recognized by the French, but they are exceptional in the aggravation of their malady to the point where social or

14. Des Esseintes' comments on Poe's treatment of the influence of fear upon the will in *Against the Grain* (p. 314) might almost be taken for an account of Conrad's description of mounting terror in *An Outcast, Lord Jim,* and *Typhoon.*

15. Aubry, *Conrad: Life and Letters,* I, 226.

16. Conrad, XXIII: *The Nigger of the Narcissus,* xii.

moral restraints no longer serve to prevent their downfall. They are test cases for a society incapable of exercising moral authority in the final issue. This is especially true of Lord Jim, who is "one of us" and whose story displays deep insight by Conrad into the problem of individual defection from an accepted standard of conduct. To this concern for the question of community sanctions as against individual irresponsibility may be attributed, also, Conrad's preoccupation with the theme of justice which emerges in *An Outcast*, carries over to *The Nigger of the Narcissus* and *Lord Jim*, and becomes dominant in the novels and stories of his middle period. The problem of the relevance of law to the special case in a changing society interested Conrad as it did his contemporaries Galsworthy and Dreiser. It continues to interest Conrad's later admirer, Graham Greene.

When mind with its traditional values loses hold in a world no longer ruled by Providence, the result is not only self-betrayal for the individual but also betrayal of man by man. The barrier between organized society and barbarism then threatens to collapse. This knowledge on Conrad's part gives rise in his work to the images of storm, flood, and explosion which charge the atmosphere with a sense of imminent disaster. Without an effective check upon individual anarchy in the form of a ruling principle to restore order and strength within the dislocated personality, collective anarchy must ensue. This view relates Conrad's studies in disintegration to the larger theme of communal instability.

Since it was, then, this intricate pattern of psychological and moral attitudes that he was attempting to convey by a method chiefly visual, one can better understand Conrad's difficulties at the outset of his career and appreciate his complaints to Garnett about the slow progress of *The Rescue.* A step-by-step examination of his work during this period shows, in fact, constant modifications in technique to meet the problem of handling such material. One of the most radical of these solutions was that introduced in "The Return," and a point of main interest in that story is not so much where it fails as why Conrad tried the experiment of supplementing analysis by concrete images.

Since it is evident that Conrad was well acquainted with the work of Flaubert when he began "The Return," it may prove helpful to refer here to a comment by the French critic, Paul Bourget, on Flaubert's method. Bourget credited that novelist with having invented a procedure of capital importance to literature in making use in *Madame Bovary* of a combination of analysis and concretion, a system of exhibiting mental activity through images on the theory that they represent the content of the mind in accordance with the doctrine of association of ideas.[17] Although Conrad is not an imitator of Flaubert, he did employ his knowledge of the French writer in the fashioning of English prose to his own ends; and it seems possible that in "The Return" he made a not very dexterous start with a method similar to that explained by Bourget.

This departure may indicate that, dissatisfied with techniques that he had previously employed as too clumsy for the kind of lengthy analysis required in "The Return," Conrad turned to a new procedure that did not fully answer his

17. Paul Bourget, "Gustave Flaubert," *Oeuvres complètes*, I, 124–25.

needs. As a result this story, by contrast with his earlier novels and tales, drags for want of action and because of the narrowed focus upon only two characters. What he seems to have abandoned temporarily was a process of psychological description through dramatic allegory, the embodiment of mental experience in concrete incident and character after the manner of Flaubert in the first *Saint-Antoine*, which Thibaudet described as "une allégorie de l'intérieur de l'homme." [18] Allegory of this sort in work before "The Return," like *Almayer's Folly*, *An Outcast*, and perhaps the early portions of *The Rescue*, required the manipulation of a heavy plot; but since it provided clear-cut visual effects, Conrad continued to use it, though, as will be shown, with greater economy.

His first novel, *Almayer's Folly* (1895), rewards attention as a leading example of the effort to present a subject from the field of morbid psychology by a method primarily dramatic and allegorical; and considering the number of clues that it offers to the interpretation of later works, it is surprising that the book has been so often taken for a mere romance of the tropics.[19] A rank overgrowth of tropical vegetation tends to smother the plot, it is true; and contrasted with the limited scope of the action, the novel is packed with character, incident, and background detail, all contributing to a confused impression on first reading. Heavy mythical and somewhat Wagnerian undertones accompany the narrative of Almayer's decline, as though the Amfortas legend had been transferred to a Klingsor's garden of Bornean

18. Albert Thibaudet, *Gustave Flaubert, 1821–1880*, p. 197.
19. See F. R. Leavis, *The Great Tradition*, p. 190.

jungle in which a Malay Parsifal, Dain Maroola, falls victim to desire and plays renegade rather than savior. Wagnerian analogies seem, in fact, to have been running in Conrad's mind; for in a letter to Mme. Poradowska he refers to the last chapter as beginning with a trio and ending in "a long *solo* for Almayer which is almost as long as Tristan's in Wagner." [20]

The first of Conrad's hermit figures, the Dutch trader Almayer, is in many ways the prototype for the rest, just as the fully described wilderness setting resembles the forest image in later stories. From start to finish the novel belongs to Almayer, an egotist who supports his own subjective universe (XI, 158); and the secondary characters are mainly agents in a visual rendering of the inner drama of his fall. Although Almayer, unlike Hervey in "The Return," has no traits of the sham priest, he maintains throughout—with his dreams, his visions of a bourgeois paradise in Amsterdam, his indifference to all women except his daughter—the appearance of a recluse; and the harsh irony of the story lies in the conspiracy of all the savage powers, the uncontrolled passions which he first tolerated and afterwards ignored, to revolt and crush this commercial anchorite.

Almayer's initial mistake, like Hervey's, derives from his loveless marriage with a native girl of whom he relieves his patron, Captain Lingard, in the hope of personal gain through the latter's favor. By this act of infidelity, a prostitution symbolized by the exchange of money and the ringing of coins throughout the book, Almayer submits himself to the wilderness and prepares the trap for his own destruc-

20. Conrad, *Letters to Poradowska,* p. 68.

tion. Failing as the manager of Lingard's trading station in the forest village of Sambir, Almayer lives only in the hope of finding gold up the Pantai River so that he can return in wealth to Europe with his half-caste daughter, Nina. But through the hatred of his wife, who plots against him with his native rivals, and through the deception practiced upon him by his ally in the gold scheme, Dain Maroola, who becomes Nina's lover, Almayer sees each of his illusions disappear. In his abandoned state, he turns from his former dreams of grandeur to those of opium and dies in the empty house that was once the symbol of his ambition.

The long passages of description make it plain that the forest in which Almayer has established his hermitage fulfills a symbolic more than a pictorial function. In one place the aspect most emphasized is the mad and brutal struggle of the plants to escape the death and decay from which they sprang and to reach the life-giving sunshine above (XI, 71). In another, young and vigorous creepers strangle giant trees (XI, 165). Passages like these reveal not only the blind and murderous striving for life but also the amazing fecundity of the vegetation, reproductive energies rioting on a bed of corruption. Exposed here is nature fallen, raw, untrammeled by any restraints of civilization or morality, a garden of death for those who cannot struggle, like the feeble Almayer who has sought paradise in nature and through a careless alliance with passions of which he was ignorant. His deterioration and the flight of Nina and Dain from the forest depths to the open sea of sunlight and life translate into human terms the drama of survival taking place in nature.

Captive thus to the wilderness and its hostile natives, his

misery at odds with his paradisal visions, Almayer suffers from the inner cleavage resulting through his separation from a familiar world. A failure of will is largely responsible for his defeat; and at the turning point of the novel, in Almayer's betrayal by his wife and Dain, Conrad develops an allegorical framework for this theme of division. From the outset Almayer is wholly dependent on the active Dain for the fulfillment of his plan of obtaining gold in order to get away from the coast, and the episode of the ruse to save Dain from capture by the Dutch authorities and to trick Almayer into believing that the young man is dead shows that this reliance amounts to identification between the two characters. In the body of the drowned boatman, disguised so as to resemble Dain, Almayer recognizes the mutilated image of his own hope of salvation projected in his Malay accomplice (XI, 99); and when he later exposes the corpse to the Dutch officers sent to arrest Dain, he speaks as though he were revealing the fact of his own death (XI, 144). The rift between Almayer and Dain is reflected in the division within Nina, whom both men desire, as she sways between a faint loyalty to her father and his white principles and the savage impulses that send her to her lover.

By this elaborate yet dramatic expedient of linking the fate of Almayer to that of the man and woman who rob him of his illusions, Conrad found an allegorical device for externalizing a concept basic to his psychology, the corruption of the will by passion. The enslavement of Dain and Nina through sensuality, which determines his own death in the wilderness, compels Almayer to witness not only the final consequences of his own original act of infidelity but also in some measure a re-enactment of the misalliance between himself and the Malay woman. Dain's active will enables him to turn with horror from the corruption in the heart of the forest awaiting Almayer (XI, 167) and to escape to the sea and to life. But the momentary triumph of the lovers when they part from Almayer in the glare of light on the island (XI, 194) is only a prelude to the suffering that will follow their increasing awareness of that difference between them hitherto veiled by the designs of nature. By contrast the figure of Almayer, for all his absurdity and weakness, acquires at the end a measure of tragic dignity which imparts a strong note of ambivalence to the conclusion of the tale with its reflections of the Schopenhauerian doctrine of life's cruelty.

All three characters fall, therefore, into the net of betrayal woven out of the inner drama of human deterioration: Almayer, a consciousness deprived of the support of will which he is impotent to control; Dain, a will corrupted by desire; Nina, a woman destined for concubinage by her father's irresolution. And although the theme of betrayal here affects the individual rather than the community, the breach of faith between Almayer and Dain, though concerned only with a gold hunt, illustrates the destruction of a bond of honor where instinct works unrestrained by a moral code.

Conrad went on to treat the disintegration of an individual in an even more minute fashion in his second novel, *An Outcast of the Islands* (1896); but in this new work, which has points of connection with *The Rescue* and its massive design, the subject becomes subordinate to an issue of greater moment. Whereas *Almayer's Folly* exhibits a subjective drama of the corrupt will, the later book illustrates the effect of such weakness upon the collapse of alliances between men in the destruction of a petty state, the little Arcadia of Sambir created in the Bornean wilderness by the adventurer, Captain Lingard. Because of the similarity in background and the reappearance of characters like Almayer and Lingard from the first novel, *An Outcast* has sometimes been regarded as a mere appendage to *Almayer's Folly;* but even a rapid comparison of plots disproves this judgment. Allowing for the inferiority of *An Outcast* in lack of concentration, profusion of detail, and occasional tediousness, the novel still shows remarkable advances in almost every department but structure. In variety of style, in its large-scale descriptive panels, in its imposing plot, the book everywhere displays, in fact, the marks of determined and fruitful experimentation.

The most notable departure is, however, Conrad's attempt to use the allegorical method of *Almayer's Folly* for a broader purpose. As the novel proceeds, the three main characters fill essential roles in what is evidently a grand parody, accompanied by the requisite cosmic sound effects, of the myth of Creation, Fall, and Judgment through a transference of the theme of *Paradise Lost* to a tropical setting. Proud of his creation of what he regards as a small Eden in the jungle, Lingard makes a place there for the Dutch clerk, Willems, whom the Captain continues to befriend even after his protégé has shown himself worthless to white society. In repayment for his benefactor's saving act, Willems, crazed by his passion for the native girl, Aïssa, opens the gates of Sambir to Lingard's trade rivals and enemies, the

Arabs, who exact this price of Willems for the return to him of his mistress. By this treachery the forces of disorder enter Lingard's world and destroy his rule. Since excess of passion motivates Willems' dealings with an infernal host in the Arabs and their leader, Abdulla, the plot of the novel contains parallels with the story of the Fall of Man. In one memorable descriptive scene, the third chapter of Part II, where the native chiefs hold a night council by torchlight to confer upon their plan to undermine the power of Lingard through the agency of Willems, the reader will recall the debate in hell in the second book of Milton's epic.

By giving Lingard a major rather than a minor role like that assigned to him in the first novel and by making him a much more assertive complement to Willems than Almayer to Dain, Conrad not only establishes a conflict more intense than that in *Almayer's Folly* but also brings the psychological theme to bear upon a wider purpose. Except for changes in treatment the deterioration of Willems corresponds to that of Almayer. Whereas the earlier book employs, however, a doubling scheme which involves Almayer and Dain, Conrad handles the problem of division and loss of will in *An Outcast* through the single character of Willems and so turns to a descriptive rather than a dramatic method. This leads to slow but thorough analysis; and in the whole of the early Conrad there are no better illustrations of the precise noting of morbid states than the seventh chapter of Part I, a minute account of the breakdown of volition as Willems succumbs to his desire for Aïssa, and the sixth of Part II, a masterful study of the paralysis of all faculties by terror in a moment of approaching death.[21] By thus concentrating upon only one character under the tyranny of the senses, by depicting so closely "the man's sudden descent into physical enslavement by an absolutely savage woman,"[22] Conrad prolonged his investigation into the malady of the isolated soul to a point beyond which he could hardly go by way of direct statement. Nina and Dain in *Almayer's Folly* are victims of passion; but Willems, having surrendered all reason, tosses like a leaf in the wind (XIV, 157). Yet throughout all his fits of craving and disgust, his intelligence remains clear and detached in the knowledge of its separation from the debased will.

The theater for this drama is again the wilderness of the first novel, the image of a fallen paradise; but here the forest, though still a place of struggle and death, is even more plainly nature under the aspect of sensual desire and hiding its perils from Willems through "the animated and brilliant flower of life," Aïssa (XIV, 76). Conrad's tone is more sardonic than in *Almayer's Folly;* for although Almayer is not altogether absurd in the wreck of his few civilized principles, Willems is ridiculous insofar as his maxims of continence and purity of heart are the fantasies of a man who believes himself ascetic but whom women pursue to the moment of his death as determinedly as the deadly sins hover about Saint Anthony. His prudery is nowhere more pitilessly mocked than in the scene from Part II wherein, re-

21. For a discussion of Conrad's use of analysis in his earliest work see Edward Crankshaw, *Joseph Conrad: Some Aspects of the Art of the Novel.*

22. Conrad, *Letters to Poradowska*, pp. 84–85.

turning from the forest after his debauch with Aïssa, he stands haggard before Almayer's verandah like "some ascetic dweller in the wilderness, finding the reward of a self-denying life in a vision of dazzling glory" (xiv, 92).

The tone of irony carries over, likewise, to the portrayal of Lingard which mingles sympathy with disparagement and thus sets a precedent for Conrad's later attitude to characters of heroic appearance but unfortunate careers. Lingard's virtues are large: his strength, his belief in life, his rectitude and firmness of will which enable him to reject the insinuation of the native politician, Babalatchi, that he murder Willems in revenge for the latter's betrayal (xiv, 238). But they are offset by lack of subtlety and by the faults of impulse, indiscriminate optimism and benevolence.[23] He has Christian traits, the heritage of the simple faith taught him in boyhood (xiv, 198); and in his support of Willems as well as in his reluctance to destroy him, mercy and charity appear to play a considerable part. Yet these vestiges of belief are subordinate to his extreme individualism and to the self-confidence which has enabled him to succeed outside organized society.[24] He is simply an adventurer with a utopian dream and the vanity of power which stimulates his pride in his Malay title, King of the Sea, and in his ability to create a kingdom on a small scale. Although he belongs to a different and better order of men than Willems, his failure to influence the latter not only points to a contrast between two radically

23. For an interesting statement by Conrad on the virtues of charity and abnegation, see *Letters to Poradowska*, p. 42.

24. Of adventurers, like Lingard, Conrad wrote in his essay "Well Done": "There is nothing more futile under the sun than a mere adventurer."—III: *Notes on Life and Letters*, 190.

opposed codes of behavior but also dramatizes the inadequacy of a personal moral standard to check action of a morbid sort.

In one great scene, as the book draws to a conclusion, the personified forces of virtue and vice clash with each other. As the psychological theme of division in *Almayer's Folly* culminates in the parting of Almayer and Dain on the island, so the psychological and moral allegory in *An Outcast* reaches its climax in Part IV with Lingard's abandonment of Willems to the solitude and bitterness of his existence with the woman whom he now detests. Clearly one of the most carefully meditated sections of the novel in its unified tone and sustained atmospheric effects—the desolation in earth and heaven, the murky light, the gathering storm—this part also conveys through an elaborate impression of cosmic disturbance a parodied version of divine judgment. Lingard, the deposed white god of Sambir, feels obliged to execute justice upon Willems; but despite the ruin of his fortunes and his utopia he is bewildered by a case of unprovoked malevolence not covered by his rough ethical code. He can find no verdict to apply to a man devoid of feelings of guilt and of any conception of honorable conduct. Fully conscious for the first time of his incompetence as lawgiver yet above the primitive impulse to kill Willems in cold blood, Lingard drops his mantle of creator and gives vent—in an episode of superb irony—to human frustration, blind rage, and wounded pride by beating the culprit with his hands, an act which redresses nothing:

> The anger of his outraged pride, the anger of his outraged heart, had gone out in the blow; and there remained nothing but the

sense of some immense infamy—of something vague, disgusting and terrible, which seemed to surround him on all sides, hover about him with shadowy and stealthy movements, like a band of assassins in the darkness of vast and unsafe places. Was there, under heaven, such a thing as justice?

(xiv, 265)

A flood of rain, like a deluge over an evil world, accompanies the departure of Lingard across the river as he turns his back finally upon the man whose life he had thought worth preserving (xiv, 284). His going takes from Willems a redeeming source of strength like that spirit of the sea with which he had always been "hopelessly at variance" (xiv, 17). But Lingard has lost as well in the collapse of his confidence in human power. In its weaving together, particularly in the judgment episode, of two of Conrad's main themes, those of justice and of man's limitation, *An Outcast* is a significant work both in itself and for the perspective that it opens on *The Nigger of the Narcissus* and *Lord Jim.*

From the forest-encircled stage of the Malayan novels Conrad turned in *The Nigger of the Narcissus* (1897) to the larger theater of human action on the sea, and by celebrating for the first time a victory of the normal over the abnormal accomplished his most affirmative allegory. The book occupies a special place in his writing, not only for its style but also for its steady vision, its heroic tone, and a general certainty both in belief and execution which carries the narrative forward with something like the determined progress of the *Narcissus* on her path homeward to the port of London. Although its spirit is not wholly serene, the tale is sustained by a note of confidence absent from the tortured self-questioning of *Lord Jim*, the nightmare vision of "Heart of Darkness," and the comic ambivalence of *Typhoon.*

Both the cosmic background and the planetary and seasonal imagery suggest a theme of exceptional scope. The sailing ship with its officers and men, voyaging alone within the circle of the horizon, is a small planet (XXIII, 29), a minute world (XXIII, 21); and the curve of the journey which begins in the darkness of the Bombay roadstead and ends, for the crew, in a flood of sunlight conforms to a pattern of life fulfilled through toil. As Conrad's most complete life-allegory the book blends psychological and moral elements to such a degree that the events of the voyage may be interpreted on the one hand with reference to individual experience, on the other to the problem of human conduct within an organized society.

By taking for his actors the company of a merchant ship governed by a traditional and proved standard of conduct rather than by abstract moral principles, Conrad brought *The Nigger* into direct relation with universal human experience and thus went beyond *An Outcast*, even though the major dramatic issue in the two books is nearly identical. Both Lingard and Captain Allistoun, as well as the mates of the *Narcissus*, are rulers; and their authority is challenged by rebellion founded upon instincts capable of reducing an ordered community to chaos. But unlike Lingard, Allistoun, the one figure in the early stories who has Conrad's unconditional respect, does not stand outside society with a self-devised code of justice. He is neither adventurer nor individualist but the rightfully invested monarch of the ship (XXIII, 31); and this knowledge of his sovereignty gives him power to win in the struggle for mastery over the crew with the negro seaman Wait, a sick tyrant and emissary from the darkness. The Captain bears responsibility not for preserving a utopian scheme but for life itself against the destructive elements in nature. Since to survive the ship's company must act as a unit indifferent to personal claims, Allistoun has to prevent division that would lead to betrayal within the group. A theme of the Malayan tales thus gains new prominence and meaning; for viewed psychologically, the Captain's effort to maintain authority over the crew is a dramatic restatement of the familiar problem of mind and will. Similarly, the other officers of the *Narcissus*, unlike the men, are incorruptible not only because they respond to the demands of life but also because their will is fixed upon an object outside themselves, the task of working the ship.

Important as an anticipation of *Lord Jim* is the fact that, by placing Wait among the crew, Conrad for the first time dealt with the influence of a pathological state upon men governed by a tried standard of conduct yet inclined to hold it in contempt. His statement in the Foreword to American readers that Wait is nothing more than the center of the ship's collective psychology (XXIII, ix) explains the portrayal of the negro in the dual aspect of seaman and grotesque embodiment of corrupt instinct. A creature from the darkness and stricken with disease, Wait appears on the deck of the *Narcissus* as if from the depths which claimed Almayer and Willems. Like these other hermit figures he too is a solitary harried by delusive or infernal visions (XXIII, 113, 127) and tormented in isolation by his particular demons, the cook and Donkin. As with Willems, fear is a symptom of Wait's deterioration, a death-fear which accompanies separation from the common affairs of men and so points the way to death itself. Although fear paralyzed Willems, terror consumes Wait and makes of him a frightened brute who evokes even Allistoun's momentary pity (XXIII, 118). The Captain has to contend directly against this evil which perverts the meaning of life, inhibits the will, and attracts the morbid interest of the crew:

> He was demoralising. Through him we were becoming highly humanised, tender, complex, excessively decadent: we understood the subtlety of his fear, sympathised with all his repulsions, shrinkings, evasions, delusions—as though we had been overcivilised, and rotten, and without any knowledge of the meaning of life. We had the air of being initiated in some infamous mysteries; we had the profound grimaces of conspirators, exchanged meaning glances, significant short words. We were inexpressibly vile and very much pleased with ourselves. (XXIII, 139)

Immured by his sole concern for himself and guarded by his deceit, Wait, though his influence remains noxious, offers only passive resistance to the will of the Captain. The active instrument of discontent in the crew is Donkin, and he grasps the opportunity presented by the quarrel over Wait to make his attack on Allistoun's life. In many respects Donkin appears the counterpart of Wait. Both are shirkers and egotists contemptuous of the rule of conduct essential to the preservation of the ship. Both are inhumanly grotesque, and the animal metaphors applied to Donkin transform him into a caricature of a man (XXIII, 110–11). But whereas Wait's contempt for his fellows is expressed mainly in words, Donkin's hatred seeks an outlet in violence. He desires to be even with everybody, and his weapon is the belaying pin (XXIII, 123).

From the psychological standpoint the connection between Wait and Donkin is important, for the perversity and nihilism of the former vents itself in Donkin's rage against all discipline. As will be shown later, especially in *Chance* where the allegorical situation is even more clearly defined, the relation between abnormality and violence is fully comprehended in Conrad's psychological thinking, for which reason the appearance of this concept in *The Nigger* is noteworthy. That Donkin should be the cause of Wait's death follows, moreover, since both have rejected communal law for that of the wilderness. In the cruel scene in the solitude of Wait's cabin, silent like the forest depths, the bird of prey settles upon the moribund animal (XXIII, 152).

As a foil to Wait among the men of the crew the gigantic and patriarchal Singleton is in some ways the most problematical figure in the book. Like the Captain whom he obeys with absolute fidelity, the old seaman is a pillar in the temple of the seafaring order (XXIII, 25), the personification of unhampered act as is shown in his unerring response at the moment of danger when the chain cable slips (XXIII, 26). But seemingly in order to make him a model of reliability in action, Conrad rooted out of his nature all but the rudiments of the mental and emotional forces involved in Wait's perverse behavior. In consequence he is at times only half-believable, a waxwork colossus. His lack of consciousness appears to have troubled Cunninghame Graham, who drew from Conrad in 1897 the reply that had Singleton been given the power to think he would have become much smaller and very unhappy.[25] Although this answer is in keeping with other reflections on mind as a burden in an irrational universe which Conrad had been writing to Cunninghame Graham from time to time in these years, it is also true that, from the viewpoint of Conrad's literary development, the reduction of Singleton to the embodiment of little more than unthinking act anticipates in an important way Conrad's later tendency to offset the corruption of will in hermit figures like Wait by introducing characters who survive in a world of evil through the possession of faculties almost as primitive as the "ragged claws" envisioned by Mr. Eliot's Prufrock. In "The End of the Tether," *Typhoon*, and "Falk" this device becomes the basis for irony which is not evident in Conrad's attitude to Singleton, whose strength forms a counterpole to the weakness of Donkin and Wait. Yet chiefly by virtue of his limitations he bulks almost too large in the design of *The Nigger*, possibly as evidence of Conrad's premonition that the standard of conduct which had formed Singleton and the rest of his generation would come to lose meaning for a world of men of a different order. Although the officers of the *Narcissus* are the finest examples of manhood in the early Conrad, they seem to represent a passing order. In enforcing a judgment of exile upon Wait and compelling the obedience of the crew, Allistoun is really no more capable of exerting moral authority over the negro than is Lingard over Willems, although he successfully re-

25. Aubry, *Conrad: Life and Letters*, I, 215.

pels the forthright evil of Donkin. Singleton, who belongs so much to the past that he has lost track of change, alone remains untouched by Wait's shadow.

The death of Wait checks, however, the trembling of the balance between good and evil; and with the resolute will of Allistoun again in full command the ship passes out of the stagnant calm to complete the voyage. All of the doubt latent in the story and voiced to some extent in the Captain's scorn for the wavering morality of the crew remains for ultimate expression in *Lord Jim* (1900), in which the standard upheld by Singleton and the officers of the *Narcissus* receives its most exacting test when applied to an individual of a type foreshadowed in the crew's demoralization under the influence of Wait. The world of the *The Nigger* is still that of the sailing ship and the book its valediction. The world of *Lord Jim* is the world of steam, of the *Patna* as well as of Brierly's crack Blue Star command, an age of new men as much as of new ships. Of this era Jim is a typical, if curious, product; and the "infernal alloy in his metal" (XXI, 45), a compound peculiar to modernity, is present also in larger quantity in the coarser metal of Almayer and Willems.

In this subtlest of all his studies in the abnormal Conrad found in Marlow, who is both analyst and confessor, a more suitable means for dealing with his material than the method of dramatic allegory used in the Malayan novels or the visual analysis employed in "The Return." A raconteur, like Conrad himself,[26] Marlow imparts to the narrative a flexibility that "The Return" never achieves. But in two crucial epi-

26. See Gordan, *Conrad: The Making of a Novelist,* p. 15.

sodes, at the height of Jim's trials on the *Patna* and at Patusan, Conrad relies upon the allegorical device to excellent effect.

The whole psychological groundwork of Jim's case has the color of a period, one in which Oscar Wilde, oddly resembling Jim to this extent, violated a moral code and afterwards refused to flee from a court sentence that left him an exile. The course of Jim's experience follows again the stages of isolation and finally total estrangement from organized mankind laid out for Conrad's earlier studies in failure. Had the story ended with his leap from the *Patna*, he would have remained only a more sensitive and well-meaning example of inner weakness which results in the double betrayal of the self and of other men. His flaw is, however, of graver consequence to an established community than that of either Almayer or Willems for the reason that he derives from the tradition of Allistoun and has been thoroughly trained for the craft of the sea. He might pass, in appearance, for one of the mates of the *Narcissus* but for a specter that shows through this fair exterior.

Jim also differs from the earlier victims of the wilderness in that his withdrawal from an ordered society is caused neither by greed nor by fraud but entirely by a temperamental aberration. In joining the *Patna* with its disreputable officers, he takes his first decisive step away from the sphere of normal activity mainly in the hope of avoiding exposure to the agony of sensations in an existence which had seemed to him unintelligent and brutal (XXI, 11). Although Almayer and Willems are likewise vulnerable through the senses, Jim's overly acute sensitivity, resulting in unhealthy nerves, is inseparable from, and in a way contributes to, his power to form ideals and to discriminate with regard to matters of honor and duty. Fine and unfortunate, with the habit of living in a mental world of romantic adventure which exceeds the possibilities of the milieu in which he is placed, he resembles, more than any of the other early characters of Conrad, people like Madame Bovary or Frederic Moreau, who, in the novels of Flaubert, become creatures of fate through excessive imagination and deficient will.

Jim's personality baffles Marlow largely because it is not one but multiple; and despite the atmosphere of mystery which the narrator creates, it is not too difficult to see Jim as afflicted by that division between mind and will which Conrad had previously studied in the Malayan novels and in broader terms in *The Nigger*. Isolated from the control of his profession, Jim discovers aboard the *Patna* that he is both idealist and dupe of instinct; and he acquires this knowledge at the expense of self-betrayal and broken faith. The episode of his temptation and fall during the accident to the ship is the greatest passage of analysis in Conrad's earlier work, comparable in its disclosure of the sudden and total disintegration of the bond between mental and volitional activity to the more discursive account of Willems' surrender to the powers of evil in *An Outcast* but far superior in its mood of unbearable tension and in the skill exhibited by Conrad in handling the scene through a satisfactory balance of the devices of analysis and visual projection so as to solve expertly the technical problem of "The Return."

The circumstances leading to the abandonment of the *Patna* all contrive, in what seems to Marlow an aimless piece of devilry (XXI, 160), to assail Jim at precisely those points where he is most vulnerable—in nerve and emotion—and, by bringing to light the breach within his nature, to reveal as well his deviation from the norm of act. The "burlesque disaster" (XXI, 121) comes to him as a complete surprise, a thing wholly outside the range of his previous experience, and hence more terrifying than the storms which drove him away from the customary routes of his profession. The incidents follow each other according to a perverse logic so that he is absorbed by a sequence of impressions as novel as those first conveyed to Willems in the solitude of the jungle. As these new sensations beat upon him, Jim undergoes his customary, but now intensified, agony of nerve culminating in the emotional exhaustion which infects his will. Marlow's comment that he was afraid not so much of death as of the emergency accurately defines his state of mind (XXI, 88). His fear results not in the impulse to self-preservation but in the wish to die in order to avoid prolonging the emotional torment. It must, therefore, be regarded as a defect of overwrought nervous feeling which does not in any way impair his courage when he faces the court of inquiry.

As his downfall progresses on the one hand by means of this attack upon his senses, it is completed on the other through mental deception. His fatal gift of "forestalling vision" (XXI, 96), of living through an experience by thought in advance of actuality, is illustrated by the way in which his mind, stimulated by emotion, creates an illusion of total disaster from the incomplete evidence presented by sense. His predictive faculty operates consistently inasmuch as the observable facts support the assumption that the *Patna* is lost. Only the final link in the actual chain of circumstances, the survival of the ship, renders the logical process absurd; and it is on this point that the mind appears to conspire with the diabolical scheme of chance to work Jim's undoing. This is the most telling example in the early Conrad of the plight of the solitary consciousness in a world not amenable to reason, of the mind in servitude to emotion and accident. The unconscious Singleton would have automatically performed the saving act of propping a bulkhead, which would have altered the balance in favor of heroism rather than cowardice.

Unable to withstand this turmoil of thought and emotion, Jim's will breaks. Yielding to the promptings of instinct, he takes to flight. One of Conrad's most brilliant strokes in psychological dramatization is his portrayal here of the lifeboat incident with the elephantine skipper and the other officers of the *Patna* struggling frantically to save their skins. The ultimate temptation on the brink of the abyss, like one of Saint Anthony's visions of evil, presents itself to Jim incarnate in these grotesque figures, Conrad's principal caricatures after Wait and Donkin in *The Nigger*. For all of his disgust Jim looks on with a kind of fascination, as Marlow points out:

> "He hadn't lost a single movement of that comic business. 'I loathed them. I hated them. I had to look at all that,' he said without emphasis, turning upon me a sombrely watchful glance. 'Was ever there any one so shamefully tried!' "
>
> (XXI, 104–5)

In these creatures of the wilderness Jim beholds the animal instincts that have been his familiars from the moment of his signing on with the pilgrim ship, and his ignorance of the dark side of his own nature reveals itself in his comment to Marlow on the difference between himself and these other outcasts (XXI, 80). By leaping into the boat with them, he cancels this difference, as Marlow knows.

The *Patna* affair as a whole, in opposing so sharply Jim's mental world of heroic ideals and the outer world of illogicality and accident, is a more complicated variation of the theme in the Malayan novels of the collapse of an artificial paradise in the midst of fallen nature. The imaginary realm, timeless and ordered, in which Jim dreams of himself as a hero and a savior contains values and fine judgments on the score of conduct which stem from a chivalric and religious tradition, perhaps the vestiges of that faith in Providence which his parson father upholds in a lukewarm manner (XXI, 5). He wants specifically to be a Christian hero, to give his life for others if need be; and the irony of his story, like that of Lingard's effort to restore Eden on a basis of savagery, lies in the fact that this attempt to transcend the brutality of existence involves him ever more deeply in the toils of a universe offering no support for such a dream. In the *Patna* half of the story, with its exposure of all of Jim's limitations, the contrast between his desire to save others and his actual abandonment of the passengers in their distress is implicit in the action; but the Patusan episode makes thoroughly plain the gulf between the ideals that he has inherited from a civilized background and the rule of survival which functions in his barbaric surroundings. When he leaves for Patusan, he becomes, in the eyes of Marlow, a hermit figure:

"It was impossible to be angry with him: I could not help a smile, and told him that in the old days people who went on like this were on the way of becoming hermits in a wilderness. 'Hermits be hanged!' he commented with engaging impulsiveness. Of course he didn't mind a wilderness...."

(XXI, 231)

Except for important modifications in atmosphere Patusan, enclosed by its wall of forest, borrows its distinctive features from the wilderness of the Malayan novels. But although the reader may approach this region of crepuscular light and silently falling darkness through the stories that precede *Lord Jim*, it is evident that the wilderness image has undergone changes relating it more closely to the almost surrealistic landscape of "Heart of Darkness" than to the fecund jungle of *Almayer's Folly*. The obvious difference in atmosphere between the *Patna* and the Patusan halves of the novel contributes to the impression that the story breaks into two parts, a division that Conrad himself admitted was the plague spot in the book.[27] But the concept of division does not seem to describe so accurately the relation between the parts, which are not really segments of one cloth, as the idea that with the opening of the Patusan narrative the key of the story is abruptly transposed from that of psychological realism to allegory. The *Patna* chapters form a necessary prelude to a more universal theme, just as the analysis of Jim's inner cleavage on the ship must precede a full understanding of his ultimate disaster. Although the Jim of the *Patna* stands as an example of a failure peculiar to modern life, the Lord Jim of the Patusan adventure becomes a more portentous figure. Symbolic for Marlow of races that have emerged

27. *Letters from Conrad*, p. 171.

from the gloom, he is likewise a symbol of man in the shadow of a gathering darkness:

"He dominated the forest, the secular gloom, the old mankind. He was like a figure set up on a pedestal, to represent in his persistent youth the power, and perhaps the virtues, of races that never grow old, that have emerged from the gloom. I don't know why he should always have appeared to me symbolic." (XXI, 265)

The great scene between Marlow and Stein in Chapter 20 which turns on the high theme of man's imperfection and tragic destiny provides the appropriate transition to events on a more exalted plane.

Cut off by the court verdict and his own scruples from the traditions of organized society, Jim seeks refuge in a world without tradition, a land without a past (XXI, 272); and his initial success as builder and governor represents the accomplishment possible to man working unaided in primitive circumstances. Conrad lays exceptional stress not only upon Jim's isolated state and upon the fact that his word alone is truth but also upon the "secular" quality of his surroundings (XXI, 265, 269). The idea of the Fall thus emerges strongly in this section of the novel and accompanies the motif of limitation very much as in *An Outcast*. Jim's defeat is, however, made to seem more ominous for mankind at large than that of Lingard at Sambir for the reason that Jim, in addition to being "one of us," exemplifies the fate in store for man in the event of a breakdown of the bond uniting a community against chaos. Amid conditions where neither the law nor the beliefs of European society prevail, Jim gains at last his opportunity to play the role of Christian hero and savior; and he becomes, like Lingard, the virtual ruler of a petty state, raises single-handed an edifice based on fallen nature, and finds himself endowed with a legend of unfailing victory and supernatural power (XXI, 266, 361). Furthermore, just as Lingard takes a central part in a parody of divine judgment, so also Jim at Patusan appears a kind of Lohengrin figure in fragmentary glimpses of a salvation myth behind the mythical-religious allusions scattered throughout this section of the novel. He descends on the court of Patusan as though from the clouds (XXI, 229), takes the death of Dain Waris upon his head (XXI, 415), and dies while heaven and earth tremble with unnatural omens which Marlow describes as though they were the epilogue to a crucifixion:

> "The sky over Patusan was blood-red, immense, streaming like an open vein. An enormous sun nestled crimson amongst the tree-tops, and the forest below had a black and forbidding face.
>
> "Tamb' Itam tells me that on that evening the aspect of the heavens was angry and frightful. I may well believe it, for I know that on that very day a cyclone passed within sixty miles of the coast, though there was hardly more than a languid stir of air in the place."
>
> (XXI, 413)

Not, however, until the arrival of the marauder, Brown, compels Jim to deliver a judgment which affects the safety of his wilderness kingdom does the full irony of his assumption of the savior's role in a fallen world become apparent; and this incident may be compared with Lingard's vain attempt to judge Willems and contrasted with Allistoun's severity towards Wait. Jim's decision to let Brown escape is, in the first place, wholly characteristic of the temperament of Conrad's hero as revealed in the *Patna* affair, the fatal gift of a personality that he tries and fails to master (XXI, 341). Through his disgrace on the *Patna* he has acquired knowledge of his divided potentialities for idealism and for submission to instinct. But the flaw in his nature remains, and the measure of self-conquest which he acquires at Patusan gives him only a respite from the specter of his weakness and the memory of his guilt. The surprise encounter with Brown, whose mad and ferocious vanity is the counterpart of Jim's refined egotism (XXI, 387), places him, therefore, in the position of the hermit assailed by the evil which he has tried to reject. Being likewise a social outcast and a leader, Brown bears a grotesque resemblance to Jim; and their meeting may be compared with the lifeboat scene on the *Patna* as the second notable example in the book of Conrad's dramatic and visual rendering of a psychological issue.

Brown's trickery succeeds because Jim, a fallible human and not the supernatural being of his legend, cannot destroy his past even in a land without a past. His faulty judgment illustrates not only the limitation of power in man that Conrad had demonstrated before in *An Outcast* but also the failure of an individual decree without the support of a general belief or tradition like that which sustained Allistoun in his contest with Wait. Jim deals with Brown, like Lingard with Willems, in accordance with a personal creed recognized by the society from which he has broken but having no relevance to the immediate needs of a secular community for self-preservation. Faithful to this detached ideal, he permits the ordered world that he has built to fall in ruins; and this fidelity makes the sacrifice of his own life both chivalrous and futile.

The strength of *Lord Jim* derives largely, therefore, from Conrad's facing of an issue which takes form in the earlier tales but which gains ultimate expression only perhaps in the nocturnal panorama of "Heart of Darkness." The crisis underlies Marlow's brooding over a question which seems to him to affect mankind's conception of itself (XXI, 93). His interest in Jim extends to the larger problem of the application of a fixed standard of conduct to the individual in every circumstance; for the fact that the standard does not hold for Jim in his supreme test on the *Patna* casts doubt upon its validity. The scene between Marlow and the French lieutenant has always been praised; and a main reason why it grips the reader is that here Marlow presses to the utmost, and without positive results, his query as to whether such a standard can be effective at all when a man, in a case like Jim's, is beyond the check of common opinion (XXI, 147). To operate successfully, the rule should enable the conflicting elements in the individual to work harmoniously to the end of purposive action; and its failure to do so for Jim on the *Patna* indicates that, when the division is absolute, man falls away from the control of the community. The one remaining safeguard is, then, perhaps a simple eye for danger like that of Singleton or of the native youth, Dain Waris, in *Lord Jim* who sees at once the evil of Brown which deceives and betrays the visionary Jim (XXI, 361). After *Lord Jim*, at any rate, characters who have this primitive eye for fact without the benefit of adequate mental resources appear more frequently in Conrad's early work.

At times in the Patusan narrative, and especially in Marlow's feelings of remoteness and nightmare, there are hints of that masterful control of an effect of distorted vision which is a primary feature of "Heart of Darkness" (1899), finished by Conrad during the writing of *Lord Jim*.[28] The impression of unreality and hallucination, which emphasizes the shock of the whole Congo experience to Marlow's mind, is greatly intensified by the violent paradoxes of the story. Both the Patusan incidents and the long African tale appear to have originated in a single revelation to Conrad of the decline of civilized man; but although at Patusan Marlow obtains a glimpse under the surface of common affairs that shakes his confidence in a world of light and order, his encounter with Kurtz is momentous enough to bring him to the point of ascetic renunciation expressed in his Buddha-like attitude on the yawl at the opening of "Heart of Darkness."[29]

Although in *Lord Jim* Conrad suggests that Patusan is relevant in a symbolic way to the contemporary world, "Heart of Darkness" remains a more universal allegory for an insecure European society; and Marlow's tale is much more than a lesson for the members of the craft of the sea. The signs of danger are evident in the gloom settling over London (XVI, 45), the funereal aspect of the city where Marlow obtains his command of the Congo steamer (XVI, 55), the contribution of all Europe to the making of Kurtz (XVI, 117). Legendary associations, even plainer here than in the

28. Gordan, *Conrad: The Making of a Novelist*, p. 260.

29. Conrad, in XVI: *Youth: A Narrative, and Two Other Stories*, 50.

earlier works, add to the "sinister resonance" of the story and to its impact on the reader's imagination. Among these, Marlow's river journey, with its analogies to a descent into the underworld, and the Tännhauser-like relationship of Kurtz to the two women, the barbaric goddess of the forest (XVI, 135) and the devoted European girl (XVI, 157), evoke an immediate response from the myth-preserving level of consciousness.

In *The Nigger* an advance from darkness to light symbolizes the process of normal life as a communal endeavor accomplished through the restraining power of a tradition. In *Lord Jim* the poles are reversed, and Jim's pursuit of the ideal becomes a flight away from the community into a wilderness where survival is the only law. A similar retrogressive movement from light to darkness, from the normal to the perverse, governs the action in "Heart of Darkness," though now the march towards barbarism involves a civilization. The African trading company, a caricature of contemporary society with its commercial and materialistic aspirations, has no purpose and no faith, no tradition, and no check upon its activities. It is merely invading nature (XVI, 76); and since anything can be done in the wilderness, it is disintegrating in an environment which knows no communal bond.

Conrad marks the progressive ruin of a once vital tradition, the decline of faith to a sham ideal of philanthropy, by his customary ironical use of religious allusions. Marlow calls himself "a lower sort of apostle" (XVI, 59); the traders appear as pilgrims with staves (XVI, 76); a round table occupies the mess hall of the company station (XVI, 74); the harlequin Russian is a "disciple" of Kurtz (XVI, 132); the cries of the natives sound like "a savage litany" (XVI, 146). This inversion of Christian symbols takes place in the new temple of primitive nature with its wall of "secular trees" (XVI, 148) wherein the high priest, Kurtz, celebrates a Black Mass (XVI, 115). The only remnant of a tradition like that upheld by Allistoun is the book on seamanship abandoned in the hut on the river bank (XVI, 99).

Bearing a certain resemblance to Wait in *The Nigger* in his grotesque and spectral appearance, Kurtz dominates the allegory as a symbol of European intelligence mastered by savagery and evil. Conrad subtly manages to suggest in Kurtz the strains of diabolism, erotic excess, nihilism, and perversity often associated with the "decadence" at the end of the century and to connect the theme of deterioration with a failure of normal love, as represented in Kurtz's intended. Conrad thus summed up in a single figure many of the traits of abnormality that he had examined in his earlier characters so that Kurtz, whose soul goes mad in solitude, becomes a chief exemplar of the hermit type. His distinction lies not only in the gulf separating his mind, which never ceases to function clearly, and his universal genius for art, poetry, and music from the corrupt will but also in his absolute conversion from the moral idealist who entered the wilderness to the agent of destruction who sinks debilitated in a ruined house surrounded by images of death. He stands as Conrad's most potent illustration of contempt for human restraints and the abuse of power through the effort to assume supernatural attributes. Having learned in his fall, however, all that Baudelaire must have known of human capacities for heaven or hell, he is superior to the blind exploiters of nature at the outer stations; and to that extent he earns Marlow's respect.

Difficult as it is to turn without some lapse of attention from this allegorical masterpiece to "The End of the Tether" (1902), the realistic tale of the sea which follows "Heart of Darkness" in the *Youth* volume, the interest of the reader quickly revives as he discovers both that the story has special merits of its own and that it restates with certain distinctive variations central themes in Conrad's first period of authorship. The hermit-like figure, representing man separated from the bonds of an established tradition, appears again in the leading character, the sixty-seven–year–old seaman, Captain Whalley; but the shift in emphasis away from the abnormal, so that Whalley's betrayal is due rather to circumstance than to any inherent weakness of nerve or will, may seem to indicate a fundamental change in the conception of the solitary type. The causes for Whalley's disaster are, nevertheless, much the same as those which produce failure in the earlier tales. By leaving a traditional order and its safeguards and risking himself in a world ruled by the law of survival, the Captain falls victim to evils which reduce him in the end to depths without a ray of saving light. Although a man of action, Whalley resembles Jim in being fine and unfortunate; and because of his knightly and aristocratic bearing, his white beard "like a silver breastplate over the awful secret of his heart" (XVI, 303), and his utter loss of an honorable name in the wilderness of rocky islands where his ship founders, his humiliation seems the least merited of all the blows that fall on Conrad's defeated men. Nowhere else, except in the *Patna* scene in *Lord Jim*, does Conrad appear more intent on demonstrating the sheer malevolence of a world of error than in this story of great and patriarchal strength driven to the defensive tactics of a cornered animal.

After a long and distinguished record as a commander of sailing ships in the East, Whalley severs his connection with an existence governed by a high standard of conduct when loss of his money in a banking crash forces him to sell his barque, the *Fair Maid*, and to become captain of the *Sofala*, an old coasting steamer owned by the chief engineer, Massy, a man corrupted by greed for funds to invest in lotteries. Although a presentiment warns Whalley that the bargain is a bad one, he agrees to share in the ownership of the *Sofala* partly because he believes that, despite his age, his sound health will enable him to serve competently for a few years more but mainly because he wants to provide help for his only daughter whose marriage to an invalid husband has compelled her to manage a Melbourne boardinghouse. His decision to pass from the old world of sail to the new one of steam and so to drift alone in the treacherous currents of modern life where individuals no longer count is important psychologically since it involves a radically altered view of human affairs and leaves him feeling "as if his very soul had been taken out of him forcibly" (XVI, 185). This sense of inward loss is comparable to that experienced by Willems in yielding to the temptation of Aïssa or to Jim's awareness of the cleft within his nature after the *Patna* crisis; for on removing from the *Fair Maid* Whalley comes to recognize capacities for evil in himself which were latent before. The determining motive in his sale of the ship, love for his daughter, begins through changed circumstances to encroach upon his strict principles of morality and duty, a conflict hitherto prevented by the undisturbed success of his career and the large freedoms of his past life.

In consenting to become the partner of a man whose passion for gambling has rendered him a dupe to fortune (XVI, 207), Whalley imagines that he can establish a compromise between his high principles and the claims of a world of brute struggle and lose only a little dignity and self-respect (XVI, 214). But when chance deprives him of his eyesight and when paternal love develops into an overmastering passion that silences the warnings of conscience, Whalley has to abandon all self-respect. He surrenders in a contest for survival which ends in the wreck of the *Sofala* through Massy's treachery and in his own death in the only ship that he has ever lost. His experience on the steamer resembles that of Jim on the *Patna* in that both men are idealists compelled to descend to the level of characters to whom honor means nothing. Massy and the mate Sterne, an ambitious schemer, are birds of prey, loyal to nothing but themselves; and Massy's absolute subservience to wilderness law is emphasized in the scene where the darkness and the odor of the tropical forest flow into his cabin below the deck:

> The ship had in that place to shave the bank so close that the gigantic wall of leaves came gliding like a shutter against the port; the darkness of the primeval forest seemed to flow into that bare cabin with the odour of rotting leaves, of sodden soil—the strong muddy smell of the living earth steaming uncovered after the passing of a deluge.
>
> (XVI, 264)

It is ironical, nevertheless, that in spite of his contempt for Massy and the difference in their moral viewpoint Whalley is partner to the engineer in guilt as much as by contract; for both are dominated by passions which lead them to place self-interest before fidelity to the ship, no matter how commendable in itself the Captain's devotion to his daughter may seem.

Still more ironical, however, by contrast to his failure under the cruelty of chance, is Whalley's strongly religious bent, his belief in Providence combined with his faith in human goodness:

> Captain Whalley believed a disposition for good existed in every man, even if the world were not a very happy place as a whole. In the wisdom of men he had not so much confidence.
>
> The disposition had to be helped up pretty sharply sometimes, he admitted. They might be silly, wrongheaded, unhappy; but naturally evil—no. There was at bottom a complete harmlessness at least....
>
> (XVI, 289)

This prominent feature of the story invites comparison again with Conrad's earlier work. A similar trust in order, backed by a more or less remote religious inspiration and a limited view of evil, found expression in Lingard and Jim; but Whalley has a positive and active faith in divine power and justice which his past experience seems to confirm (XVI, 271). In no other tale by the early Conrad is the issue between religion and scepticism so openly debated as in the conversations between Whalley and his friend, Van Wyk, the young Dutch planter who has adopted a cynical attitude of detachment from society; and all of Whalley's defense of Providence fails to explain the insane logic of his own tragic downfall. Like Jim's belief in a world suited to the exploits of a Christian hero, the Captain's faith seems to derive from a peculiarity of temperament, his natural vigor and active disposition (XVI, 293); and whereas this religiosity is an inherent part of the man's fine simplicity and rectitude, which the discriminating Van Wyk admires, it also stimulates unwarranted trust in himself and a consequent ignorance of evil in insidious forms.

To survive, however, Whalley needs clear sight more than faith, and the approach of blindness provides an especially bitter denial of his optimism. The descent of this wholly unforeseen affliction manifests a kind of perverse cunning behind events comparable to that exhibited in the design of the mock disaster that overwhelms Jim on the *Patna*. Neither the Captain's religion nor his ideal of duty sustains him in his reaction to this physical injury. Instead he forsakes his moral integrity and bends his mind to contriving the deception by which the eyes of his Malay steersman are made to compensate for his own loss. The mind thus becomes subservient to the organ of sight; and the story, which is replete with ocular images from the opening page description of the dazzling light blinding the eye as the *Sofala* moves toward the bar in the river, brings to fullest development the theme of vision introduced from time to time in earlier tales.

The main clue to this theme, realized in character, can be found in the portrayal of the Malay serang, upon whose sharp sight Whalley depends for the carrying out of his ruse. The eyes of the steersman are compared to the lens of a camera and his mind to a "sensitized plate" having no apparatus for speculation (XVI, 228). Hence although unlike the white men he has no intellectual mistrust of his senses, which give him accurate and precise knowledge, he is incapable of comprehending the simplest motives of his superiors (xvi, 228). This one-sidedness is, however, less morally detrimental than the deceit practiced by the officers of the *Sofala;* for by self-interest and passion they falsify both the evidence of their senses—Massy and Sterne being able to see well enough through Whalley's trick—and their interpretation of motives, whereas the Malay remains wholly loyal. Nothing distorts his exact perception, just as nothing stands between Allistoun's quick glance at Donkin's belaying pin or Singleton's at the chain cable and their capacity to act. This treatment of the division of mind and sense which marks "The End of the Tether" looks forward to the handling of the same problem in a spirit of ironic comedy in two important stories at the end of this phase in Conrad's career, *Typhoon* and "Falk."

In the brilliantly designed *Typhoon* (1902), written just after "The End of the Tether," the motif of vision occurs again in relation to Captain MacWhirr, whose extraordinary eye for fact and literal mind are reminiscent of the primitive mental equipment of Whalley's serang. But the theme appears in a subtler context than that of the preceding story; and Conrad's remark in the Author's Note on the "deep conviction" (xx, ix) with which he approached the subject verifies the impression that *Typhoon*, though brief, ranks with his major work. Like *The Nigger*, *Lord Jim*, and "Heart of Darkness," *Typhoon* reaches a high plane of allegory in its development of the familiar subject of man's limitation in a world of evil.

The hurricane, which hurls destruction upon the *Nan-Shan* with all the fury of a cannonade (xx, 91), is the most malevolent of all the storms in Conrad; and its full terror is kept constantly before the mind of the reader by repeated images of cataclysm. These deluge metaphors, strongly reminiscent of those employed in *An Outcast*, *The Nigger*, and *Lord Jim*, are supplemented by images of violent passion to make the gale a composite symbol of both natural and human evil (xx, 19). In its effort to drive MacWhirr's ship over the edge of the world (xx, 74), the typhoon attacks like a personal enemy (xx, 40) and with the force of an explosion, a cataract, or a trampling mob (xx, 90):

> It was something formidable and swift, like the sudden smashing of a vial of wrath. It seemed to explode all round the ship with an overpowering concussion and a rush of great waters, as if an immense dam had been blown up to windward. In an instant the men lost touch of each other. This is the disintegrating power of a great wind: it isolates one from one's kind. An earthquake, a landslip, an avalanche, overtake a man incidentally, as it were—without passion. A furious gale attacks him like a personal enemy, tries to grasp his limbs, fastens upon his mind, seeks to rout his very spirit out of him.
>
> (xx, 40)

Conrad's key image of the wilderness, separating man from an ordered world, takes a new form in the circular typhoon; and MacWhirr's decision to head the *Nan-Shan* and her shipload of coolies into this heart of darkness corresponds to that initial step into the wilderness with which the action of so many of the early stories begins. But although *Typhoon* conforms thus to the general pattern of so much of the work of Conrad's first phase, it is distinguished both by its tone, which is satirical throughout, and by the skillful method employed to convey the point of the satire by indirection.

Bluntly stated, the theme of *Typhoon* is a version of Conrad's major topic of the limitation of human nature, or of the isolated individual when confronted by evil from outside his experience or beyond the protection of the community. Conrad develops the theme, however, by the dramatically successful interplay of two characters, Jukes and MacWhirr; and the clue to the story lies in an understanding not only of their relationship but also of the special function assigned to MacWhirr. Although associated as members of the seaman's craft, the two men are in everything else extreme opposites.

The mate of the *Nan-Shan*, young Jukes, a sociable person with a normal share of good sense, imagination, and sympathy, represents average humanity. He is a competent officer who is temporarily overcome by fear only when he is exposed to the fury of the typhoon which he would have avoided had the decision been his and not MacWhirr's. The analysis of his collapse during the storm corresponds generally with the longer passages on the effects of terror in *An Outcast* and *Lord Jim* (xx, 51–53), and because of the similarity in their temptation and fall Jukes appears at first sight only a more commonplace Jim. Actually, however, they differ in that Jim fails while seeking to escape the trials of his profession whereas Jukes is so much bound to the traditions of the sea that he is amazed by MacWhirr's refusal to take a simple precautionary measure to ensure the safety of the ship and the people aboard. His world is confined by the reasonable man's concept of order; and when he is forced into a situation quite unrelated to his idea of what the worst should be, he not surprisingly reaches the point where, as the French lieutenant says in *Lord Jim*, one "lets go everything."

Whereas Jukes conforms, then, to the mean of human nature, MacWhirr is so exceptional in his unerring response to fact as to border on the impossible; and one can readily accept Conrad's statement that the Captain was never seen in the flesh (xx, viii). With his remarkable eye for defective door locks he represents an excess of the empirical as much as earlier characters, like Almayer, illustrate an extreme in visionary habit; and his complete dependence on what he can actually see, which is the mark of his originality, is accompanied by a lack of imagination great enough to isolate him from the commonplace world of people like his wife and Jukes (xx, 4). Although this very deficiency accounts for his dauntless temperament, it also leaves him tinged with absurdity; for his magnificent display of courage during the storm is wasted effort fom the standpoint of common sense. His determination to take the ship through the storm rather than to deviate from her course is preposterous, based as it is upon contempt for the inherited wisdom of the craft of the sea contained in the book on storms (xx, 33). Yet the fault is not willful indifference to tradition, since in every other respect MacWhirr is faithful to the standards of his trade. The error results from a failure of the predictive faculty which is a safeguard to Jukes with his modicum of imagination. Without MacWhirr, Jukes could not have survived the hurricane and the ordeal of initiation that he undergoes, precisely because the test is utterly beyond normal human capacities for endurance.

MacWhirr's purpose in the story is clarified, therefore, when he is seen both as a measure of the limitations of the average man, Jukes, and as a warning of what is required of the individual who expects, as Kurtz expected, to survive evils outside the communal frontier. Only on condition, in other words, that man can equal MacWhirr by a radical transformation of his very nature dare he risk an encounter with the unknown and the powers of darkness. For a moment in the typhoon Jukes and MacWhirr are bound together, but their temporary alliance only emphasizes their separation in all normal circumstances. At the height of the story Conrad again calls, therefore, upon his device of dramatic allegory to strengthen the point of what must certainly be regarded as one of the great short masterpieces of irony in English literature.

Leading out from this basic structural counterpoise of Jukes and MacWhirr, strands of irony run through *Typhoon* from beginning to end. Understandable in the light of Conrad's purpose is the use made, for example, of the type of parody on salvation and judgment developed more elaborately in *An Outcast*, *Lord Jim*, and "Heart of Darkness." There is a comic element in the fact that the storm is compared to a phenomenon that might accompany the Day of Judgment (xx, 44) and that the complacent MacWhirr manages to put this "elemental fury into its proper place" (xx, viii). As a hero fit for a world of accident, the Captain, in one place, appears before the barometer as "a booted and misshapen pagan burning incense before the oracle of a Joss" (xx, 84). In a crisis beyond the reach of human rational and predictive powers and on the assumption that chance governs the universe, MacWhirr acquires almost superhuman stature, because his absolute reliance on immediate fact adapts him thoroughly to such an unprovidential scheme. He is, nevertheless, a creature of chance with a Damoclean sword above his head (xx, 86); for his survival depends ultimately upon a whim of fortune. The final shaft of Conrad's irony strikes at MacWhirr's equal distribution of the silver dollars among the coolies at the end of the voyage (xx, 102), an act in keeping with the Captain's rough notions of justice formed, like Lingard's, beyond the pale of custom. Although honest in its way and perhaps the most that can be expected in a lawless world, this primitive division of property is poor recompense for the grievance of the Chinese, the force of which Jukes recognizes by arming the crew with rifles.

The strongly ambivalent quality of *Typhoon* results from the adoption by Conrad of a semicomic attitude to the problem of individual divergence from a norm of conduct; and in this story, with its unwavering control of a small but perfectly chosen set of materials, he arrived at his most compact and lucid expression of the idea of man's limitation. Whereas in the earlier stories the downfall of the solitary in the wilderness had been presented as a fairly straightforward record of defeat within a surrounding frame of irony, Conrad, in *Typhoon*, completed a work ironical at the core and in the hypothetical character of MacWhirr portrayed a hero who triumphs by virtue of deficiency. A similar ambivalence and sardonic humor pervades "Falk" (1903), the only other long story in the *Typhoon* volume; but this tale with its strident colors, primitive people, and almost too perceptible odor of flesh does not match its predecessor in intellectual subtlety.

Notable, however, is the fact that from his pathetic and inarticulate hero, the Scandinavian tugboat skipper, Falk,

Conrad stripped away all of the moral and intellectual refinements of civilized man in order to permit the one basic desire for life to exist as a single force. Feeling no tie with organized society (xx, 198) and concerned only with preserving "the five senses of his body" (xx, 199), Falk has survived, because he was the best man in a life-and-death struggle, the experience of cannibalism in which he shared on a derelict cargo steamer after all feelings of solidarity between the men had gone (xx, 231). Still burdened with this memory of ten years' standing, Falk, now an Eastern river pilot, cleanses his guilt in the tears of compassion that flow from the eyes of the woman who accepts his love, the silent and statuesque niece of Hermann, a fatherly German ship's captain whose notions of civic virtue are outraged by the knowledge of Falk's misfortune. The last view of the lovers, standing like two pagan deities in a flood of sunlight (xx, 239), is reminiscent of the departure of Dain and Nina in *Almayer's Folly* in that life prevails over all conventional principles of right and wrong. In "Falk," however, the Schopenhauerian implications are less pessimistic than in Conrad's first novel; and love acquires the status of a bond against the world's cruelty that it holds so frequently in his later work.

Falk is the last character in Conrad's early writing to be described explicitly as a hermit:

> The girl, with her hands raised before her pale eyes, was threading her needle. He glanced at her and his mighty trunk overshadowed the table, bringing nearer to us the breadth of his shoulders, the thickness of his neck, and that incongruous, anchorite head, burnt in the desert, hollowed and lean as if by

excesses of vigils and fasting. His beard flowed downwards, out of sight, between the brown hands gripping the edge of the table, and his persistent glance made sombre by the wide dilations of the pupils, fascinated.

(xx, 217–18)

Yet, his appearance to the contrary, Falk is no ascetic. The guise of a hermit is no more appropriate to him than it is to Willems; and this fact has more than comic significance. By suffering in the wilderness, by the indignity of eating human flesh, Falk wears the mask of the anchorite as a token of deformity, of the wound of division between his conscience and the instincts which have caused his fall. His desperate longing for the love of Hermann's niece is evidence of his desire to rid himself of this stigma and to regain his feeling of solidarity with mankind. Because of his simplicity he survives the division which destroys earlier characters and exerts his will to live.

He survives, nevertheless, through a heavy sacrifice of distinctively human attributes. His primitive valor and the physical splendor of the girl stand out against a background of violence and cruelty in the midst of which the image of a broken temple, the group of stony islets associated with the memory of Falk's disaster, appears to symbolize the fall of a tradition into something resembling "the heaps of a cyclopean ruin on a plain" (xx, 209). In this environment, where suffering is inevitable, the only alternatives to Falk's blind will to exist and to perpetuate life are the Biedermeier morality of Hermann, whose floating Arcadia with its children and clotheslines is innocent of the wickedness of the sea (xx, 149), and the Buddhist temple representing annihilation (xx, 210). Conrad seems, therefore, to concede the victory of the normal over the abnormal with a slight toss of his hands.

As distinguished from the more civilized failures who precede them, the heroes of *Typhoon* and "Falk" do, then, emerge battered from their contest with the powers of darkness. Their survival depends, however, upon conditions which are made to seem impossible for the man endowed with an average measure of imagination or reason; and in having little or no contact with the generality of mankind, they are pitiful. They are strange men, perhaps supermen, but in any case lopsided in that their strength derives from acuity of the senses rather than the mind. Since they do not break in the wilderness under the strain of internal conflict, the conclusion suggested by their experience is that only armed with qualities, more godlike or bestial, that exceed the ordinary human standard dares man venture to penetrate the unknown.

At the close of his first period of authorship Conrad had moved, therefore, from the depiction of men who cannot become heroes to that of heroes who are not quite men; and this is evidence enough that he worked not haphazardly from one story to another but under the stimulus of a coherent body of intuitions and convictions that went very deep into causes for uncertainty in his age. The peculiar ironies and tensions that develop with the progress of his writing show, however, that it is necessary to approach whatever is positive in his viewpoint by way of a screen of seemingly negative reactions. Produced at a time of crisis and transition in moral and social values, his work impresses the reader not by a statement of faith or of a few elementary moral precepts but rather by a half-scornful acceptance of the results of a sweeping away of beliefs. This attitude explains in great part the emphasis upon deterioration, the reversal of traditional symbols, the ironical basis in so many of his stories. It also accounts for the lack of confidence in man outwardly manifested in his general treatment of character. Only a few of the men in his early work seem capable of enduring the trials of existence without having sacrificed some essential feature of their humanity; and these characters, the captain and mates of the *Narcissus* or the officers of the *Judea* in "Youth," are members of a craft with an inherited standard of conduct which is disappearing with their generation. Yet a code of behavior no longer valid for people of a different age may serve as a contrast to an inferior ethic which supplants it, and the nonexistent ideal of man complete and assured of his place within an ordered society may be held as a norm by which deviations from it can be judged. Such an ideal, it appears, was native to Conrad's thought, even though as an artist concerned with contemporary subject matter he drew men who were incomplete and withdrawn from the communal orbit. His humanistic spirit finds utterance in his comment on Willems and Aïssa in their utter solitude and despair at the end of *An Outcast:* "They both long to have a significance in the order of nature or of society." [30]

Conrad had no high opinion of man's significance apart from a background of order which conferred human status upon him; but since the early stories emphasize the absence of order in nature and its possible breakdown in society, the

30. *Letters from Conrad*, p. 42.

problem of how man is to remain human or whether, after all, he needs to becomes crucial. For Conrad, man is severely limited, prone to evil rather than good; and the whole point of much of the irony in the work of this period is that in attempting to transcend his humble state the individual is thrust back into full awareness of his limitations or down to a level below the human. In another reference to *An Outcast* Conrad pointed out that "Willems fails in his effort to throw off the trammels of earth and heaven," [31] and the same remark could be applied to Kurtz in "Heart of Darkness." As a rebuke to pride the image of the Fall reappears steadily in Conrad's tales, usually accompanied by that of the wilderness which is symbolic not only of the loss of Eden but also of the outer and inner terrors disclosed to the man who does not share in the burden of toil. But it is noteworthy that these images are not completed according to Biblical pattern, for there is no promise of ultimate relief or divine consolation to man in his fallen state. In this partial myth Providence seems to have no role, and humiliation lies in store for men who try to assume that part themselves. The wilderness is not merely a desert to be made fruitful. It is chaos: the realm of chance, irrationality, and brute survival which accords with the grimmer interpretations of a materialistic world-picture. Alone in this waste man has, literally, no chance insofar as he is merely human. Both his mind and his senses can become servants of the irrational when he is overcome by the "Dark Powers." This dilemma, in which man falls into evils worse than those decreed for Adam and inexplicable without a Providence to blame, is not far re-

31. *Ibid.*, p. 42.

moved from the thought of Hardy in his blacker moods. It also lies at the base of Conrad's ironies as well as of his tolerance for the man who in his failure bears witness to fundamental injustice in the design of the universe.

This conception of the wilderness helps to account for Conrad's attitude to the hermit figure, the most original feature of his imagery in this phase. Adapting a familiar symbol in the French literature that he knew, Conrad gave the hermit a key function in the development of his own theme of limitation. From Flaubert's device of representing Anthony's temptations as concrete personages in an allegorical drama, Conrad seems to have obtained the hint for the objective treatment of psychological and moral conflict, of the division between mind and passion, which he used in climactic scenes in his earlier work and never afterwards abandoned completely. But the hermit figure is much more than an instrument in his method. With the French the character had come to stand, either in a serious or a semicomic light, for a pose of contempt towards bourgeois life which expressed a peculiarity of modern temperament. Conrad likewise stressed at times the temperamental peculiarities of the type. Many of his hermits—Almayer, Willems, Wait, Jim, Kurtz—are men whose mental or spiritual aberrations cause them to deviate from a norm of conduct. But for Conrad, with the possible exception of Hervey in "The Return," the anchorite is not an agent of anti-bourgeois satire but a figure who, in his retreat, offers a challenge to a ruling principle of order. By a system of contrasts—setting Willems against Lingard, Wait against Allistoun, Jim against the fraternity of seamen—Conrad gave dramatic expression to moral and social tensions in his age which, because unresolved, allowed for a play of reciprocal irony. But in this balance of forces the weight of the irony lies heaviest upon the hermit as a departure from the implied norm of limited man in an ordered society. In his withdrawal the anchorite becomes a victim of extremes, of the division which ensues when man tries to cast off the trammels of his middle state. He envisions paradise at the moment when he sinks deepest into the toils of the wilderness. Once again, therefore, Conrad engages in an ironical reversal of an image from a Christian background with the apparent intention of a gibe at Providence for the disorderly state of creation. Retirement to a wilderness for ascetic or contemplative purposes can be justified only on the premise that God dwells in solitary places. When, instead, the wilderness is left abandoned to the strife of savage instincts, the ascetic ideal becomes absurd and the hermit himself a prey to the evils which he seeks to reject.

Closely bound in with this view of the anchorite and his perils are the main elements of Conrad's psychological equipment which, in keeping with its time, centers in the question of will and its failure. As a result of the disturbance to his humanity involved in the division between mind and instinct, the solitary finds himself incapable of acting when that is necessary to survival. A Schopenhauerian tendency to negation enters into the detachment of Flaubert's hermit; [32] and in the light of Conrad's dark picture of the wilderness his occasional mistrust of the will to live, with its burden of human frustration, is not surprising. Despite notes

32. See Baillot, *Influence de la philosophie de Schopenhauer*, p. 218.

of cynicism in tales like *Almayer's Folly*, "The End of the Tether," and "Falk" it is difficult, however, to regard Conrad as an advocate of detachment. His stories imply the necessity for action even when they demonstrate its impossibility in adverse circumstances or in certain types of character. But, characteristically, he seldom portrays the norm of successful act but rather deviations from it in extremes of passivity, like that of Almayer, or of automatic response, as in Singleton. The problem of will forms a part of the larger issue of the survival of man as a human being, and the theme of action and negation continued to attract Conrad until he came to full grips with the subject in *Victory*.

It is in great part due to his discovery in the first stage of his literary career of his principal themes and of his characteristic methods, including that of allegory, that Conrad's early work must always seem vital to his reputation. The vision of life to which he gave form at this time was to remain, scarcely modified, as the source of his later writing; and it is doubtful whether he afterwards expressed it with greater force or economy of means. Yet it would be unjust to praise the achievement of this period at the expense of the technical mastery of his later books wherein he extended his range as a creator of character and scene. From a strictly literary viewpoint he succeeded best in his early work with the short novel and story. Tales like "Youth," "Heart of Darkness," *Typhoon,* and "Amy Foster" are rarely surpassed by later products of the same genre. He was not yet, however, an expert craftsman in the full-scale novel. Structurally, *An Outcast* and *Lord Jim,* though provocative in content, are imperfectly massed. His improvement in the long novel is, however, a notable feature of his second stage of authorship where he turned at the same time from his contemplation of the predicament of man as an individual to that of society in which man should fulfill his limited task.

Chapter 3

THE INCENDIARY

Man in Society

THE storm in *Typhoon* drives in its final assault on the *Nan-Shan* with "the throb as of many drums in it," with "the chant of a trampling multitude" (xx, 90). The ship reels as though battered by a mob. This metaphor carries, perhaps, a germ of that idea of modern society tottering from the shock of forces released by the weakness and folly of men which matures in Conrad's second period of authorship.

In the Author's Note to *Nostromo* Conrad states that after he had finished the *Typhoon* stories there seemed nothing left to write about and that, his first wave of creative energy having subsided, his inspiration underwent a change:

> I don't mean to say that I became then conscious of any impending change in my mentality and in my attitude towards the tasks of my writing life. And perhaps there was never any change, except in that mysterious, extraneous thing which has nothing to do with the theories of art; a subtle change in the

nature of the inspiration; a phenomenon for which I can not in any way be held responsible. What, however, did cause me some concern was that after finishing the last story of the "Typhoon" volume it seemed somehow that there was nothing in the world to write about.

(IX, vii)

The "anxiously meditated" *Nostromo*, the first of his novels with a distinctly political emphasis, bore evidence of the direction which the change was to take; and the inspiration held over a period which included the two intricate works, *The Secret Agent* and *Under Western Eyes*, the stories in *A Set of Six* that reflect the mood of the novels, and that curious book—at once credo, treatise on aesthetics, and paean to heroes—*The Mirror of the Sea*. The period closed for Conrad in physical exhaustion, the severe illness which sprang up "like a tiger in the jungle" after the last words of *Under Western Eyes* had been written,[1] and from which he recovered to embark on the homeward passage to popular success that came at last with *Chance*.

The recent appearance of books like *Nostromo* and *Under Western Eyes* in moderately priced editions gives evidence of a centering of general interest on this work of his great middle stage. But this wider response has developed slowly, and Conrad had reason to complain that his writing in these years gained scant appreciation and little understanding from the public in his day. His abrupt departure from the sea background of his earlier tales no doubt confused and disappointed readers who had misunderstood the real aims of his first efforts in literature; and although the

1. Conrad, XIX: *'Twixt Land and Sea*, vii–viii.

themes that had occupied him from the time of *Almayer's Folly* survived the change in his inspiration, they acquired new significance in the rich and varied settings of the novels of the second period. For the first time and, on the whole, for the last he became almost exclusively a novelist with a critical vision of contemporary European society. He had been so, by implication, from the opening of his career; but not until *Nostromo* did he raise his eyes from the solitary individual to a world in turmoil.

His work at this stage seems the product more of invention and conscious skill, less autobiographical and symbolic, than that written earlier, as may be seen in the labored effect of the weaker stories in *A Set of Six*. Yet in its balance between finished craftsmanship and keen insight it shows increasing mastery. Conrad himself remarked to J. H. Retinger that of all his books he considered *Nostromo* and *The Secret Agent* the best because in these he overcame successfully "the most difficult technical obstacles." [2] Respect for this judgment grows with the reader's full acquaintance with these novels as well as with *Under Western Eyes*, for long one of his most neglected books but a triumph alone in the maintenance of an atmosphere peculiar to the tale.

In viewing the contemporary world, Conrad found applicable again his familiar conception of life as divided between the realm of chance and brute struggle and that of human ideals of order and value. Failure occurs, once more, through man's defeat by insurgent passion or instinct. The arena for this contest in the novels and in many of the stories in *A Set of Six* is a scene of violence, cruelty, and

2. J. H. Retinger, *Conrad and His Contemporaries*, p. 107.

madness: the South American seaboard convulsed by warfare and factional discontent in *Nostromo* and "Gaspar Ruiz," the London underworld breeding crime and anarchism in *The Secret Agent*, the Russian capital paralyzed by terrorism and revolutionary plots in *Under Western Eyes*. In this explosive atmosphere virtues are effaced and the worst passions inflamed, often by the acts of a corrupt officialdom.

This chaos is sometimes emphasized by contrast with a mountain image of rest and concord, remote and unattainable: the white dome of Higuerota dwarfing the soldiery at battle in *Nostromo* (IX, 27), the peaks of the Cordilleras lighted by sunset above the darkness on the bodies of the executed men in "Gaspar Ruiz,"[3] the snow-covered chain of Jura watched by Natalia Haldin as she dreams of an era of peace in *Under Western Eyes* (XXII, 104). The mountains stand apart from a world where bonds between men have fallen apart and where forces potentially good are wasted, just as the strength of the guerrilla fighter, Gaspar Ruiz, turns to a destructive end when made instrumental to the hatred of his royalist wife in the struggle for South American independence. Except for changes in setting, this world of strife resembles the wilderness of fallen nature in the Malayan tales, a treacherous foundation upon which men build temporary social and legal institutions. Based in a morass of evil, the edifice of the modern state is bulkier but hardly more secure than the trading post in the jungle.

In European society Conrad detected a process of decay spreading into the upper levels. He recognized also the dan-

3. Conrad, in XVIII: *A Set of Six*, 20.

ger of a rift between social classes when elements of discontent and irrationality flame up through the shell of civilization. Anarchism threatens not from outside society nor from economic struggle but from the spiritual laxity of all members of the community who acquiesce in or encourage tendencies making for their own ruin. For this reason Conrad's frequent portraits of anarchists almost invariably demonstrate that such characters are motivated not by ideas but by inner weakness. In the story, "An Anarchist," from *A Set of Six* (1908), for example, the French workman, Paul, becomes a convict and an exile because in a drunken moment his weak head fails to control his impulse to shout "Vive l'anarchie" in a café (XVIII, 147). For Conrad true anarchy is the will for self-destruction.

Two other tales in *A Set of Six* have upper-class characters who seem unable to cope with violence because they have been sheltered too long from active experience of coarser emotions. The narrator in "The Informer," a story slightly reminiscent of parts of *The Secret Agent*, is a refined collector of frangible art objects who knows no passion other than that for gathering bronzes and porcelains and to whom everything violent appears unreal (XVIII, 77). He entertains a Mr. X, a radical journalist and inspirer of anarchistic societies, who preaches that the amendment of mankind must come through terror and destruction. With his bony face Mr. X is an incarnation of madness and death; yet he fascinates his host as a kind of rare monster, a collector's item (XVIII, 76).

Mr. X tells the story of the daughter of a government official who plays at anarchism in order to cultivate unfamiliar emotions and to assert her individuality. Her pretense involves her in real tragedy, however, and costs the life of a man who betrays himself in the mistaken belief that he is protecting her. Apparently the art collector fails to see that the anecdote applies to him even when his guest caps the grim joke by remarking that people like the girl are fated to perish:

> "Don't you know yet," he said, "that an idle and selfish class loves to see mischief being made, even if it is made at its own expense? Its own life being all a matter of pose and gesture, it is unable to realize the power and the danger of a real movement and of words that have no sham meaning. It is all fun and sentiment. It is sufficient, for instance, to point out the attitude of the old French aristocracy towards the philosophers whose words were preparing the Great Revolution."
>
> (XVIII, 78)

The second of these two stories and the finest in the volume, "Il Conde," deals with an old European nobleman with a rheumatic ailment which compels him to live quietly in Naples. The Count is a lonely man, gracious, kindly, and honorable, whose entire life has been regulated by the conventions of his class and freed from any rough contacts with the world (XVIII, 272). While walking one evening in the shaded alley of an amusement park, he is assaulted by a South Italian youth with an expression of peevish discontent, who presses a knife to the Count's stomach and demands that his victim give up some personal articles of small value. The attack is sheerly irrational; and unable to recover from being treated with gross contempt, the Count virtually commits suicide by leaving Naples.

Unlike the narrator in "The Informer" the Count is a sympathetic figure, one of Conrad's most memorable studies of an aristocrat. Among other things the story illustrates the fact that not even the kindly man at the threshold of death is certain of being spared the indignities of a world of accident. The Count represents, nevertheless, a form of subtle egotism, an overrefinement of feeling, which prefers death to the disturbance of a notion of propriety. He has grown complacent in the belief that existence is secure. What destroys him is not so much the insult as the sudden upsurge in him of powerful and hitherto dormant emotions. All of these forgotten passions appear to take form in the person of his assailant, whom the Count seems to recognize (xviii, 280). An unexpected revelation of unknown terrors bewilders the Count in a situation similar to that of Jim on the *Patna*. He is typical of Conrad's fine characters in that he is both chivalric and absurd, noble and vain, in his choice of death as an escape from humiliation. The story has symbolic overtones; for as the Count, haunted by the face of the young ruffian, leaves Naples, the reader has a momentary glimpse of civilization falling before the barbarian.

The foregoing characters suffer from the division portrayed by Conrad in his earlier work, but they have special status as members of a leisure class unfitted for survival. From this point on Conrad deals frequently, but not always convincingly, with people of this kind; and in his concern with them he reveals doubt regarding the soundness of European society. His outlook is modified, however, by his lack of faith in improvement through the extension of human power or through radical schemes for political reform.

This belief had shown itself indirectly before in his ironic treatment of utopian projects in *An Outcast*, *Lord Jim*, and "Heart of Darkness." But his distrust of political change accomplished by force becomes outspoken in many of the novels and tales beginning with *Nostromo*. In *The Secret Agent* he insists, for example, that "the way of even the most justifiable revolutions is prepared by personal impulses disguised into creeds" (XIII, 81), and in the Author's Note to *Under Western Eyes* that no fundamental change of hearts follows the downfall of any given human institutions (XXII, x). Such views can, of course, be regarded as the outcome of his idea of man as a limited being. If man is fallible and easily corrupted, his abstract beliefs may be the product of irrational motives.

As a development, therefore, of his earlier habit of mind Conrad traced social weakness to moral and psychological causes. It is worth noting, however, that whereas during his first period he had, with some misgivings, suggested that the seafaring order to which he paid tribute in *The Nigger*, *Lord Jim*, and "Youth" approximated a communal ideal, he came to exhibit no such trust in European forms of government with their routine systems of authority. As a result more importance attaches, in the writing of the middle phase, to the claims of the individual divided between the opposing forces of a rigid official code of morality and law and a world ruled by chance. When subject to accident and the drive of instinct man must err, and existing moral and legal institutions no longer supported by faith offer him little safeguard. Mindful of this dilemma Conrad laid increasing weight upon the need for a bond of sympathy or love which the individual requires for protection in the absence of such a principle in modern society—a morality of feeling without which justice becomes no more than an instrument of vengeance, as in the case of Jim. In "Falk" Conrad had touched on the redeeming power of sympathy in the love of Hermann's niece for the suffering mariner in a tale slightly reminiscent of Wagner's *Flying Dutchman* theme; but in his later work love, or more commonly its denial by characters overtaken by misfortune, becomes a main feature.

Although love and faith provide, therefore, the only dependable check to the perils of chance, this bulwark is difficult to establish against the counterclaim of the self-preservative instinct and its impulse to betrayal. Understanding and respect for the human bond make possible a balance of the contradictory motives of love and self-preservation, whereas the supremacy of instinct leads to moral failure. This assumption governs the dramatic issue, in which love is repressed or perverted through the dominance of convention or of instinct, in the three novels and in many of the short stories of Conrad's second phase. The value of loyalty to a bond of feeling as an element of man's essential humanity is set forth positively, however, in "The Duel," one of the lighter tales in *A Set of Six*, where the conflict lies between sentiment and honor and the powers of irrationality and self-regard. The Napoleonic setting is important, since the mutual faith of a comradeship of arms and dedication to an adventure of epic scope unite the principal characters, cavalry officers of the Grand Army.

The story begins, like others by Conrad, with the plunge of a reasonable man into an absurd situation which carries with it the risk of life. The hero, D'Hubert, a northerner, has a calm temperament that finds all absurdity distasteful (XVIII, 206); and the duel forced upon him by his Gascon comrade, Feraud, who is irrational and subject to caprice, is not only dangerous but also quite inexplicable. The alternatives open to D'Hubert are either to escape the imbroglio by reporting it to his superiors or to continue to jeopardize his life and his career indefinitely in a series of contests with his challenger. On three occasions he refuses to rid himself of Feraud by permitting the law to interfere, even though the third summons to fight, delivered on the eve of D'Hubert's marriage, offers the greatest provocation for turning the vain hothead over to the police. Before going out to this last and most futile encounter, D'Hubert tastes and masters every emotion of fear and repugnance (XVIII, 248); but after defeating Feraud and compelling him to make peace, he feels that life has been robbed of its charm because it is no longer menaced (XVIII, 259). The outcome of this ridiculous conflict is self-knowledge for D'Hubert and a revelation of the sincerity of his fiancée's love.

Though amusing, the story is also significant in its portrayal of one of Conrad's few successful heroes, a man who does not fall before the passions represented by Feraud even though he has to contend with irrationality in its crudest form. Two factors override the counsels of prudence and self-preservation: D'Hubert's adherence to the code of honor governing the duel, and his kindness and strong sense of comradeship (XVIII, 167). Sentiment causes him to respect the humanity of an individual as savage as Feraud and thus to maintain the bond between men in a world of

chance. The troublesome duel becomes an initiation into all of the emotions; and through his refusal to betray himself by betraying his enemy, D'Hubert survives as a moral being. Although his adventure has its ironic side, he emerges from the solitary trial armored for life, unlike the art collector in "The Informer" or the Count in "Il Conde" who have lost acquaintance with the coarser emotions.

The related themes of chance, law, and initiation make "The Duel" resemble Conrad's more difficult tale, "The Secret Sharer." Although he published this story in 1912, Conrad had been meditating upon its germinal idea for a good many years so that the work may be considered here as relating in an important way to the present discussion. No one of his later pieces of short fiction has been examined more attentively by critics, and though narrower in scope than *The Nigger* it may also be construed as a life-allegory in terms of the homeward voyage of a ship under an inexperienced captain whose future depends on the accomplishment of his task. No other story illustrates better Conrad's interest in the struggle of the individual to come to terms with himself and with external reality.

In the opening pages the intense and ominous stillness over sea and land and the absence of all motion create the atmosphere of utter solitude which surrounds the young Captain.[4] Being a stranger not only to the ship and crew only recently placed under his command but also to himself (XIX, 93–94), he is attempting by introspection to acquire a measure of certainty, the strain of which labor is emphasized by the restless movement of his eyes vainly exploring the

4. Conrad, in XIX: *'Twixt Land and Sea*, 92.

horizon for something on which to settle (XIX, 91–92). As in earlier writings like "The End of the Tether" the motif of vision figures prominently in "The Secret Sharer"; and from this first reference to the eye staring into space, the narrative proceeds to the final concentration of sight on the hat left behind in the water by Leggatt, a "saving mark for the eyes" (XIX, 143).

The Captain not only lacks self-knowledge but also harbors a false sense of security and, like Jim, an ideal conception of his own personality (XIX, 94). He takes confidence in the notion that the sea has no surprises for his discomfiture, that he is secure in a life without annoying problems (XIX, 96). While convincing himself of his safety, however, he dismisses the anchor watch and takes that duty himself, a capricious act which results in a blow to his serenity and assurance. By obeying this impulse and so making unavoidable his encounter with Leggatt, the mate and escaping prisoner from the nearby ship *Sephora*, the Captain, like D'Hubert in "The Duel," finds himself involved in a chain of circumstances which make plain the distance between the ideal and the actual in conduct.

The shock of discovering Leggatt swimming alone in the sea gives the Captain both visual proof that the world is not secure and also an image of that side of his own nature which is immersed in the same dark waters. In consequence he feels identified with Leggatt and accepts without hesitation the latter's story of having killed one of the crew of the *Sephora* under the stress of passion during a storm. Leggatt's danger thus conveys a warning not only of the Captain's own limitations, already glimpsed by the reader in the matter of the anchor watch, but also of the peril of self-idealization in a world hostile to ideals. This disclosure of the conflicting tendencies in man leads to the feeling of duality which brings the Captain near the point of madness (XIX, 130). The psychological aspect of his dilemma merges with the moral problem of helping a man guilty of a crime according to social convention. In aiding Leggatt, he acts in accordance with necessity and with the instinct of sympathy; yet the partnership between the two men, which enables the Captain to obtain self-knowledge, also stands in the way of his approach to familiarity with his ship. His erratic behavior in keeping Leggatt concealed makes him suspect in the eyes of the crew.

This situation reaches a climax in the scene between the Captain and Archbold, the master of the *Sephora*, when the latter arrives in search of his missing captive. The alternatives before the Captain here are like those presented to D'Hubert in his quarrel with Feraud: to surrender Leggatt to punishment at the cost of human feeling or to protect him at the risk of the Captain's whole future. Archbold completes, therefore, the main triad of characters who figure in the allegory of conventional and private justice. He appears to represent a narrow creed of vengeance at variance with conditions in a world of accident. He seems to the Captain dull and tenacious in a spiritless way in his desire to turn Leggatt over to authority despite the fact that the mate's courageous performance during the storm has saved the ship:

His obscure tenacity on that point had in it something incomprehensible and a little awful; something, as it were, mystical, quite apart from his anxiety that he should not be suspected of "countenancing any doings of that sort." Seven-and-thirty virtuous years at sea, of which over twenty of immaculate command, and the last fifteen in the *Sephora*, seemed to have laid him under some pitiless obligation.

(XIX, 118–19)

Yet Archbold stands for the law on the *Sephora* (XIX, 107); and in taking sides with Leggatt against him, the Captain disobeys a mandate of established legality in favor of a personal code which recognizes the common bond between men in their submission to error. The incident is timed expertly to occur at the moment when the Captain's efforts to hide Leggatt have strained his endurance to the utmost and thus to emphasize the full burden of choice that oppresses modern man caught in a state of divided loyalties. Like D'Hubert, the Captain comes to the verge of disaster in fulfilling his pact with Leggatt and in acquiring knowledge of human capacities for strength and weakness. Yet the hat which he gives Leggatt as a token of pity saves him and his ship under the shadows of Koh-Ring and marks his acceptance of the concrete fact that determines action.

Both "The Duel" and "The Secret Sharer" provide an introduction to the three major novels of Conrad's middle period in that the scheme of the action in all is the progress of a train of circumstances which, set in motion by an impulsive or irrational act, moves swiftly and according to a perverse logic of its own towards a disastrous end. The short stories halt at the brink of a fatal conclusion, whereas the novels press forward to a tragic denouement. Conrad's adoption of this somewhat melodramatic pattern of linked incidents backlashing towards catastrophe, a device used to good effect by later authors such as Fitzgerald in *The Great Gatsby* and Graham Greene in *The Heart of the Matter*, helped to provide his middle novels with a structural tautness lacking in those of the earlier phase. But this design also made prominent a leading theme in *Nostromo*, *The Secret Agent*, and *Under Western Eyes;* for in these books the death-directed movement of chance proceeds without arrest from a moral barrier in society or a bond of love or sympathy between individuals.

This chain of fatality is most clearly evident in the structure of *Nostromo* (1904), which, despite its technical complexity and rich fabric of events, develops according to a basically simple logic of plot. Christopher Isherwood, the British novelist, has recently commended *Nostromo* for its still lifelike picture of a backward South American state; [5] but although setting and character conform faithfully to a particular milieu, the story reflects Conrad's outlook on the state of contemporary European society as well. Realistic though it is in detail, the book has a kind of legendary breadth of outline. By his decision to reopen the San Tomé silver mine against the warnings of his father, who had died hating this concession forced upon him by a corrupt government, Charles Gould, the English administrator, allows the poison of the silver to drain into the already tainted whirlpool of political life in Costaguana and so brings evil upon himself as well as the rest of the principal characters. A revolution ensues, and in the course of this upheaval Gould takes steps to maintain the security of the mine which

5. Christopher Isherwood, *The Condor and the Cows*, p. 5.

in the end brings financial prosperity to the state at a high cost of individual suffering to those who have participated in the change. The curse attached to the silver is as productive of fatal consequences as that upon the stolen gold in Wagner's *Ring*, for avarice not only defeats the protagonists in the novel but also excludes love as a redeeming force. Linked with the spiritual distress of Gould and the ruin of Decoud, the boulevardier and sceptic, and Nostromo, the Italian captain of Cargadores, are the grief-stricken figures of their women, Emily Gould, Antonia Avellanos, and Linda Viola, sacrificed to the modern "religion of silver and iron" (IX, 71). Love as a corrective to tragic error is eulogized more forthrightly in *Nostromo* than in the other books of this phase; and neglected though it is, it stands forth as the single value transcending the egotism of a materialistic world. At the end of the novel the storm created by the passions of men subsides to give place to the image of the solitary Linda tending the light above the darkness in which lies the treasure of the mine:

> The whole refracting apparatus, with its brass fittings and rings of prisms, glittered and sparkled like a dome-shaped shrine of diamonds, containing not a lamp, but some sacred flame, dominating the sea. And Linda, the keeper, in black, with a pale face, drooped low in a wooden chair, alone with her jealousy, far above the shames and passions of the earth.
>
> (IX, 552)

The shadows cast upon the idea of material progress and upon the sufficiency of the individual make *Nostromo* in essence a great morality play in modern costume on the theme of human limitation. The long descriptive passages at the opening serve not only to set the stage for a drama international in scale but also to contrast the magnificence of the natural scene with the trivial designs of the actors who make their appearance in a noise of rifle fire and runaway horses (IX, 27). The state of perpetual revolution in Costaguana is one of meaningless struggle in a fallen world where ideals of peace and concord are as remote as the white shoulder of Higuerota from the searching eyes of old Viola, once a follower of Garibaldi but now past the humanitarian dream of his youth, and where those who devote themselves to right and justice die, like the patriot Don José Avellanos, worn out with the lifelong effort (IX, 477). As in "Heart of Darkness" the invasion of the "temple of nature" (IX, 3) has plunder for its aim so that the sanctuary becomes transformed into a pit for mutual destruction.

The humblest witness to human deficiencies is Hirsch, the forgotten and disregarded hide exporter, whose cowardice makes him a memorable, if simple, addition to Conrad's studies in fear. His torn body, left hanging by the revolutionists in the gloom of the customhouse (IX, 427), is one of the products of Charles Gould's attempt to throw wealth into the scale of justice and represents as well a betrayal of life through ungoverned passion in Sotillo, a leader of the insurgents who kills Hirsch out of avaricious rage for possession of the silver. But the one forthright critic of excessive confidence in men is Doctor Monygham, the medical officer of the San Tomé mine, whose distrust of motives is the outcome of his own moral disaster under an earlier dictatorship when he learned, through torture, that pain severe enough will obliterate the values of truth, honor, and self-respect

(IX, 373). Out of this experience, the extreme test—like that of Jim on the *Patna*—which proves that there is no limit to the humiliation which a man can be made to endure, has come his inveterate opposition to reform (IX, 370), his distrust of political idealists like Gould (IX, 376), and his conviction that the last thing a man should trust is himself:

> Charles Gould rode on, and the engineer-in-chief followed the doctor indoors.
>
> "That man is calmness personified," he said appreciatively.... "He must be extremely sure of himself."
>
> "If that's all he is sure of, then he is sure of nothing," said the doctor.... "It is the last thing a man ought to be sure of."
>
> (IX, 310)

The Doctor's love for Emily Gould, in whom sentiment and the wisdom of the heart take precedence over intellect (IX, 67), manifests his belief that in sympathy alone can man expect help. His final pronouncement on the whole San Tomé enterprise also reflects his humane temperament and disillusioned eye for fact:

> There is no peace and no rest in the development of material interests. They have their law, and their justice. But it is founded on expediency, and is inhuman; it is without rectitude, without the continuity and the force that can be found only in a moral principle.
>
> (IX, 511)

Monygham's condemnation of blindness and arrogance weighs heavily upon Charles Gould, a representative Conradian figure both heroic and absurd in his fidelity to an ideal which proves illusory and in his ignorance of the insidious effect of emotion upon judgment. In these qualities he is a recognizable, though more affluent, successor to the men of chivalrous bearing in the early stories. Conrad seems, however, to have drawn upon his lifelong interest in the Don of Cervantes in portraying this English adventurer in capitalism; [6] for Gould is quixotic in his aims and in his knightly demeanor as exhibited in his gravity and ascetic habits, in his brilliant horsemanship of which the jingle of spurs through the halls of the Casa Gould is a constant reminder (IX, 73), and even in the sword of wealth which—drawn in the interest of order and justice—proves such a double-edged weapon in his hands (IX, 365).

In his ambition to employ the power and wealth that he derives through working the mine to found an ordered world upon the hotbed of evil in Costaguana, Gould resembles the Lingard of *An Outcast.* Like Lingard this "Idealist-creator of Material Interests" (IX, xi) is really no more than an adventurer (IX, 365), and his utopian dream leads him directly to a paradise of snakes which the mine has become after its abandonment by his father:

> . . . his wife and himself, after a tortuous ride through a strip of forest, had reined in their horses near the stream, and had gazed for the first time upon the jungle-grown solitude of the gorge. The head of a palm rose here and there. In a high ravine round the corner of the San Tomé mountain (which is square like a blockhouse) the thread of a slender waterfall flashed

6. Conrad became familiar with *Don Quixote* in his boyhood, and in his work he refers several times to Cervantes' hero. The quixotic figure, like that of Gould, is usually treated with a measure of irony. Although Conrad recognizes the charm of the Don, he looks ironically upon the mission of that "redresser of this world's wrongs." See especially VI: *A Personal Record*, 36–37, 44, 71; III: *Notes on Life and Letters*, 61–62.

bright and glassy through the dark green of the heavy fronds of tree-ferns. Don Pépé, in attendance, rode up, and, stretching his arm up the gorge, had declared with mock solemnity, "Behold the very paradise of snakes, señora."

(IX, 105)

This view of the wilderness does nothing, however, to weaken Gould's enthusiasm for his project. The illusion which blinds him to his own faulty judgment, as it drives Lingard to display impotence in the judicial faculty, is his confidence in Abstract Justice, of which the thriving mine becomes a symbol (IX, 402). Irony lies in the fact that the logic of events proceeding from Gould's original linking up of justice with wealth does move inexorably towards the establishment of a kind of permanent justice, which is, as Monygham says, inhuman and without rectitude. The mine in the end reigns secure in a tyranny more pitiless than the government of the Costaguana politicos, and the road to this ultimate triumph of justice is marked by a waste of human lives, including that of Gould himself who becomes the slave rather than the master of the silver.

The flaw in his otherwise impeccable character is not so much, however, that Gould confuses end and means through an error in reasoning as that his pinning of faith to material interests is in its origin a choice into which rationality does not seem to enter at all. In his decision to reclaim the mine, he never knows his real motives which spring from the "round-about logic of emotion" (IX, 85). In the scene in the ruined Italian palazzo where Emily consents to go with him to Costaguana as his wife, Gould starts the mechanism of fatal events which runs on to the sacrifice of their love to his own consuming passion for an idea. His motionless staring at the cracked marble urn is "tense and irrational," the look of a man "who elects to stare at nothing past a young girl's head" (IX, 63). From this point on he becomes helplessly involved in the consequences of the step that he has taken and faster bound to the abstraction that his wife recognizes as evidence of insanity, of a will haunted by a fixed idea:

> Mrs. Gould watched his abstraction with dread. It was a domestic and frightful phenomenon that darkened and chilled the house for her like a thundercloud passing over the sun. Charles Gould's fits of abstraction depicted the energetic concentration of a will haunted by a fixed idea. A man haunted by a fixed idea is insane. He is dangerous even if that idea is an idea of justice; for may he not bring the heaven down pitilessly upon a loved head?
>
> (IX, 379)

The image of stone that appears frequently in Conrad's work, apparently to represent life frozen through a decline in human feeling, applies to Gould in his association with the marble urn and the statue of the kingly rider that he passes on the road in Costaguana (IX, 48). Shut off behind a wall of silver, he hardens like the glare in his room (IX, 209), ends sterile like the silver itself (IX, 522). All of his finer qualities and inherent power are warped by the inner division between his "conscious and subconscious intentions" (IX, 378).

Although Gould retains a certain regal dignity to mask his spiritual desolation, Martin Decoud, the second to perish in the trio of exceptional men in the novel, is less outwardly imposing since he exemplifies the failure of "intellectual audacity" (IX, 501). With a sceptical temperament more thoroughgoing than that of Van Wyk in "The End of the Tether," Decoud has spent most of his youth as a dilettante (IX, 153). When he undertakes with Nostromo to save the lighter of silver from capture by the revolutionists, he enters upon an action which proves fatal to him, since the unfamiliar surroundings of the Placid Gulf make the analytical play of his thought useless as a protection against the terrors of darkness and solitude. He is, therefore, a new and remarkable example of Conrad's theme of the limitation of mind in a world without order or faith. In ordinary circumstances his sharp intelligence enables him to see at once the confusion of motives, the impossible alliance of "Don Quixote and Sancho Panza, chivalry and materialism," in the national character of Costaguana (IX, 171). Capable of avoiding the mistakes of an idealist like Gould, he is incapable of Monygham's fidelity to anything outside himself; and when the Placid Gulf offers nothing to the grasp of his intellect, his thoughts, like those of Jim on the *Patna*, spin in a closed circle (IX, 277) in a void beyond the world of sensation in which he believes (IX, 229). This section of the novel and its sequel in Decoud's suicide in the loneliness of the island make up one of Conrad's greatest studies in the pathological effects of isolation for a civilized mentality lacking in self-knowledge.

With the moral ruin of Nostromo, whose tragedy embraces that of Viola and his daughters, the train of fatal necessity touched off by Gould's ambition burns down to the level of the common people and flames out in domestic drama. Gould's belief that money-making can be justified because it brings security and afterwards a better justice to the people (IX, 84) is refuted in the collapse of Viola's household and the degeneration of Nostromo who, creeping on all fours through the jungly ravine that hides the treasure (IX, 542), becomes the last inheritor of a fallen paradise opened by the exploitation of nature. Although as the "Great Man of the People" (IX, xiii) Nostromo embodies a heroic image to accord with the bent of the popular imagination, he ends, like Gould and Decoud, an example of wasted powers not only because he permits himself, through his craving for prestige, to be used as an instrument for futile aims but also because his exaggerated self-confidence makes him a "victim of the disenchanted vanity which is the reward of audacious action" (IX, 501).

Neither the exotic setting in *Nostromo* nor its stage crowded with action and character conceals the irony of life sacrificed to the utopian ambition to create order on a basis of material progress. Were it not for Conrad's skillful employment of varying points of view so as to prevent monotony in the line of the narrative, the operation of fate in counteracting the illusions of freedom and idealism in limited men would seem mechanical; for the heads of Gould, Decoud, and Nostromo fall almost in a fixed order. In the novel which followed soon after *Nostromo*,[7] *The Secret Agent* (1907), the judgment of society remains much the same; but Conrad arrives at a vision of impending chaos which brings to the surface strange elements from depths of the imagination hardly stirred, perhaps, since "Heart of Darkness." In consequence *The Secret Agent* presents a

7. Conrad, XIII: *The Secret Agent*, ix.

more complicated and less immediately perceptible set of internal relationships than the more conventionally planned *Nostromo*. Criticism has already seized upon some of the notable aspects of the book: the fact that it is Conrad's first novel dealing with a European city and with the underworld of London, that it is masterly in its ironical method and sustained atmosphere wherein the prevailing tone of squalid darkness is from time to time pierced by a glare of gaslight and reddened with blood. But it is possible to go further and to recognize that this atmosphere provides the visual medium for transmitting an impression of horror following upon a glimpse under the familiar surface of life like that experienced by Marlow in *Lord Jim* and by Kurtz in "Heart of Darkness" and granted again here to Winnie Verloc in her "tragic suspicion that 'life doesn't stand much looking into' " (XIII, xiii).

Whereas in *Nostromo* overconfidence in human power and the neglect of personal bonds leads to individual disaster, the world in *The Secret Agent* appears stricken with moral insanity which breaks out in the incomprehensible attack upon the fifth meridian, the Greenwich Park bombing incident.[8] Conrad's catastrophic vision turns Victorian London not only into a jungle where man preys upon his fellows but also into a slimy aquarium, the breeding place of monsters (XIII, 147). Many of the characters are grotesque as though they expressed in deformity of body a perversity of soul, caricatures of the same order as Wait in *The Nigger* or the

8. For a report on the actual attempt to bomb the Greenwich Observatory and on the death of the culprit, see Ford Madox Ford, *Memories and Impressions*, p. 136.

Captain of the *Patna* in *Lord Jim*. In such a world the idiot Stevie, who can at least feel pain, becomes a kind of hero. The circles that he draws for amusement suggest cosmic chaos (XIII, 45) and thus stand as an adequate device for a society in which he can appear both as the only victim of the Greenwich Park affair and as part-avenger of the crime.

This effect of pervasive moral corruption which makes society powerless to nullify the destructive results of the insane will to do violence sets *The Secret Agent* apart from the crime or police story which it resembles only superficially. Though it may be considered, furthermore, to possess some of the characteristics of the hunted-man novel, as written in recent years by authors like Graham Greene and F. L. Green, it displays little of the continued pressure of excitement that marks the narrative of flight. The melodramatic features of the story are confined mainly to the materials selected by Conrad to form what, in summary, appears a simple plot. Frightened by a threat of loss of employment with the foreign embassy which pays him for occasional work as a secret agent, the middle-aged Verloc, in public the keeper of a shop trading in immoral goods of one kind or another [9] and serving as a meeting place for anarchists, takes seriously the proposal of the secretary, Vladimir, that he attempt to blow up the Greenwich Observatory. Keep-

9. In his play based upon the novel, Conrad apparently decided to make clear to the theater audience the nature of the "doubtful wares" in Verloc's shop. In the following speech, Vladimir says to Verloc: "It seems to me that you are dealing in revolutionary literature and obscene photographs. I suppose you find it a good combination. Intellectual indecency and that other kind." See Conrad, *The Secret Agent: A Drama in Three Acts*, pp. 22–23.

ing his intentions hidden from his young wife, Winnie, Verloc bungles the scheme so that the only real harm done is to Stevie, Winnie's brother, the idiotic boy who is killed by the explosive that Verloc has given him to carry. The police investigation carried on by the Assistant Commissioner and Inspector Heat is officially successful; but it fails to uncover the moral and psychological grounds for a crime which results in actuality from social evil and from an absence of faith between individuals as represented by the loveless marriage between Verloc and his wife.

A powder train of fatal events set alight by a purely irrational deed again determines the action in *The Secret Agent*. The impact of the story is, however, more alarming than that of *Nostromo* not only because the tragic issue comes so swiftly and with such explosive results but also because the whole chain of consequences defies the logic of thought. In the fact that ordinary reason cannot comprehend the dialectic of evil, that "perverse unreason has its own logical processes" (XIII, x), lies the true horror of the tale. Feraud's attack upon D'Hubert in "The Duel" is a dangerous absurdity, but the caprice which motivates it derives ultimately from a whim of temperament. The basic motives for Gould's decision in *Nostromo* to reopen the mine are irrational; but they are, nevertheless, cloaked by an ideal honorable in itself. But the initial cause for disaster in *The Secret Agent*, Vladimir's impulse to incite Verloc to bomb the Observatory, is purely insane. The act itself, as Vladimir says, must appear mad:

"But what is one to say to an act of destructive ferocity so absurd as to be incomprehensible, inexplicable, almost unthinkable; in fact, mad? Madness alone is truly terrifying, inasmuch as you cannot placate it either by threats, persuasion, or bribes." (XIII, 33)

This argument and its acceptance by Verloc, Vladimir's equal in moral insensibility, are symptoms of impending ruin in society. The signs of total disaster, of explosion, wreckage, and shambles, are much more prominent in *The Secret Agent* than in *Nostromo* and more ominous in that the scene is a European capital and not a South American state. The causes for unrest Conrad attributes, however, not to the activities of professional radicals but to the anarchistic spirit throughout the social order. The proclaimed anarchists—Michaelis, Yundt, and Ossipon—are, as Conrad remarked in a letter to Cunninghame Graham, not revolutionaries but shams; [10] and they are treated as mere parasites, bloodthirsty in speech but incapable of striking an effective blow for a proletarian cause which they enjoy contemplating in the abstract. They are, inherently, no more vicious than the elderly patroness of Michaelis, who believes in the complete economic ruin of the system which permits the indulgence of her eccentricities (XIII, 111), who is enabled by her wealth to intimidate the Police Commissioner, and who—like the narrator in "The Informer"—is fascinated by an ex-criminal. Since organized radicalism appears, therefore, as but the reflection of the half-conscious conniving of a society in its own fall, anarchism masquerading as respectability—in the Secretary of State and Inspector Heat as well as in Verloc and Vladimir—engages in mock combat with anarchism in the guise of proletarian doctrine; and the opponents mu-

10. G. Jean-Aubry, *Joseph Conrad: Life and Letters*, II, 60.

tually tolerate and prey upon each other, often to the cost of the innocent.

An ironical device for stressing fundamental resemblances between characters of this sort, one mentioned in Conrad's stage directions for the play version of the novel,[11] is that of creating physical similarities between, for example, Verloc and Heat, both of whom are obese—a system of correspondences designed apparently to indicate an overgrowth of flesh with an impoverishment of spirit. Throughout the novel there is a preponderance of sheer bulk, an impression of inert masses without inner force to quench the flame of irrationality burning through the social framework. This weight betokens helplessness before peril just as the rheumatic affliction of the Count in "Il Conde" is a token of the inner paralysis which makes him vulnerable to the irrational attack of the Camorrista.

The true symbol of the nihilistic tendencies under the cover of prevailing convention is the Professor, the megalomaniac from whose private store of explosives Verloc obtains the materials for the Greenwich bomb. Like Mr. X in "The Informer" the Professor makes no reservations in his belief in wholesale destruction as a guiding principle. He is central to the novel; for he influences the two main spheres of action, the world of administrators and police on the one hand and the underworld of the Verlocs and their kind on the other, and commands the fearful subservience of both. The

11. See Conrad, *The Secret Agent: A Drama in Three Acts*, p. 143. In his stage directions for III, iii, Conrad says of Heat and Verloc: "There is a certain similarity in their personal appearance—both big men, clothes same sort of cut, dark blue overcoats and round hats on."

terror which he inspires in the policeman, Heat, no less than in the radical, Ossipon, emanates from the perversely simple logic of his thought that life, in all its complexity, can offer no defense against the will bent on death. This iron faith puts him beyond all means of coercion except violence and risk of life for his opponent. Yet he is a product of the society that he seeks to annihilate, a supreme example of the individualism of Gould or Nostromo rendered fanatical. The thwarted vanity of this former scientific materialist (XIII, 80) shapes his obsessive dream of a world in shambles where only he remains, if he is strong enough (XIII, 304), with his motto, "No God, no master" (XIII, 306).

The absence of a moral bond to enable society to resist disintegration is illustrated in the indecisive conflict waged between the Professor and the legal hierarchy of police and administration, a stalemate in which the Professor, bound by no rules, is ready at any moment to sweep the pieces from the board. The great theme of justice, as an encounter between an unwieldy system of law and convention and the insurgent force of irrationality, which can be traced in Conrad's work from the opposition between Lingard and Willems, Allistoun and Wait, the maritime court and Jim on through the failure of Gould's ideal of equity, is lifted in *The Secret Agent* to greater prominence, since the contest, with legality now clearly on the defensive, has become desperate. The question is no longer how justice can be made to apply to the individual beyond the social pale but rather how it can survive in a world yielding everywhere to the rule of unreason which operates according to its own inhuman law.

The fixed idea of the Professor is "to open the first crack

in the imposing front of the great edifice of legal conceptions sheltering the atrocious injustice of society" (XIII, 80); and there is nothing to block its fulfillment. The edifice that he desires to shatter—having no stronger defenders than Heat, a slave to routine; the Police Commissioner, an energetic but officially hampered Don Quixote (XIII, 115); and the Secretary of State, a weak-eyed crusader in a frock coat (XIII, 138)—is supported precariously over the black waters of crime into which the Commissioner descends in his solitary pursuit of Verloc. The same impression of tenacity without active moral conviction given by Archbold in "The Secret Sharer" is present here in a whole bureaucratic system, though it is most evident in Heat, who is cowed by the Professor's insane purpose because it lies outside the closed circle of police methods and ideas:

> The mind of Chief Inspector Heat was inaccessible to ideas of revolt. But his thieves were not rebels. . . . And Chief Inspector Heat, arrested within six paces of the anarchist nick-named the Professor, gave a thought of regret to the world of thieves—sane, without morbid ideals, working by routine, respectful of constituted authorities, free from all taint of hate and despair. (XIII, 92–93)

The activities of police and administration in attempting to solve the crime at Greenwich consist merely in following the clue, the scrap of cloth from Stevie's overcoat, placed in their hands by pure accident after the explosion and leading back no farther than the miserable home of the Verlocs, who are as much fettered by the chain of necessity as their pursuers. In the end the exposure of Verloc solves nothing important. Fate runs its course to the extermination of Winnie, whereas the real criminal, the Professor, goes free by tacit consent of the police.

The finely integrated design of the novel becomes apparent when due account is taken of the pivotal function of the scrap from Stevie's overcoat with the address printed on it by his sister to avoid his getting lost. This fact, at first disregarded, not only links the domestic tragedy of the Verlocs with the more comprehensive tragedy of justice but also serves to short-circuit the current of circumstance so that the main explosion, the upshot of Vladimir's ferocious joke, occurs not at Greenwich but in the heart of the Verloc household when Winnie kills her husband. It is further significant that the fragment of cloth, which survives all efforts at secrecy and counts more in the final reckoning than all the logic of officialdom, comes into existence as the result of the one genuine act of love in the story, Winnie's passionate concern for her brother's life. But this same act, implicated in a mesh of deception, contributes to the play of fate as it comes to an end in the murder of Verloc, the suicide of Winnie, and the mental deterioration of Ossipon, Winnie's intended lover. Hence love, which should offer a bond against the conspiracies of accident, is here not only disregarded but perverted so that sources of life in Winnie are rooted out more violently than the same energies in *Nostromo*. For this reason *The Secret Agent* is, as Conrad indicated, before all Winnie's story (XIII, xii). Cast away at the end in the dark waters of the Channel, she cries out for life, a victim in the fatal recoil of her own capacity for love.

In *The Secret Agent*, as in *Nostromo*, love is sacrificed to material purposes, since Winnie, for the sake of her mother and Stevie, sells herself to a man repugnant to her for the silver coins in the till of the shop of doubtful wares. But the betrayal of love, which in *Nostromo* begins with the somewhat impersonal transference of Gould's affection from his wife to the mine, is connected in *The Secret Agent* with that division in Winnie of passion from sex which is relieved only by her killing of Verloc after he has confessed to her his part in her brother's death. All of her maternal desire, struggling unnoticed beneath the stony calm of her domestic existence, is transferred from Verloc to Stevie; and the latter's disappearance removes this frail safeguard to the bargain between husband and wife. Being a completely emotional creature of magnified pity and compassion, Stevie becomes an overcharged receptacle not only for the instincts repressed by Winnie yet exposed in her sewing of the address inside his coat but also of all those impulses of the heart which a society grown feeble presses into the depths to await the igniting current of fate. Stevie does, therefore, "turn up with a vengeance" (XIII, 230); for as Winnie advances to stab Verloc, it is Stevie whom she resembles, as it is also Eros denied who guides the blow: "As if the homeless soul of Stevie had flown for shelter straight to the breast of his sister, guardian, and protector, the resemblance of her face with that of her brother grew at every step, even to the droop of the lower lip, even to the slight divergence of the eyes" (XIII, 262).

As Conrad wrote to Galsworthy in 1921 with reference to the dramatic version of the novel, the subject of *The Secret Agent* "does not lend itself to exact definition." [12] The

12. Aubry, *Conrad: Life and Letters,* II, 258.

whole meaning of the book lies as much in its atmosphere of suffocating darkness, its imagery of ruin and flood, as in the delicately woven design. But the main intention seems apparent, most of all, perhaps, in the cry of horror from the inarticulate Winnie at the realization of her doom. The keynote of the book, sounded in the title, is secrecy: the concealment of truth and of misery under a lid of convention as represented not only by Verloc's shop front hiding his commerce in shady wares but also by the more imposing front of law and diplomacy covering an even shadier traffic in venality and crime. It is above all a secrecy which muffles the fact of human betrayal and the contempt for human values that make social failure a moral rather than an economic or scientific issue.

Like the other novels of this period as well as much of Conrad's earlier work, *The Secret Agent* dwells upon the failure rather than the triumph of positive values so that love becomes a destructive rather than a redeeming force. The inversion of normal ideals is, however, so extreme in *Under Western Eyes* (1911) that only the faintest line separates irony from cynicism; and the story moves to a conclusion which seems inevitable yet utterly barren of human good. Within the special atmosphere of the Russian and Genevan setting, the leading theme is, nevertheless, similar to that in the two earlier novels. The action turns on the denial of love and sympathy in a corrupt social environment, the despotism of Vladimir in *The Secret Agent* written large in the autocracy of Czarist Russia, and the ultimate acknowledgment of these virtues in circumstances of atrocious cruelty. In contrast, however, to the books preceding it,

Under Western Eyes is primarily a story of intellectuals who are in direct touch with conflicting ideologies; and for this reason it conforms to the usual definition of a political novel. But the story, as the title indicates, is set within a broader frame of reflection on differences between Western and Eastern mentality, ethics, and conduct; and in this respect the use of an Englishman for narrator, a language teacher who speaks for a Western point of view, serves not only to lend distance to a tale of spiritual ruin in a hopeless political situation but also to remind the reader of the existence of habits of life other than those which prevail in the action.

In accordance with Conrad's usual procedure in the work of this phase, the novel builds upon the consequences of an act determined by irrational motives. When Victor Haldin, a young opponent of tyranny who has just assassinated a particularly odious Russian minister, suddenly enters the room of Razumov, a poor university student who hopes by his own efforts to make a career as a scholar, and asks the latter to aid him in escaping from the city, Razumov taken by surprise at first appears to consent. But later, while wandering in the streets after a vain attempt to deliver a message for Haldin, he is overcome by fear; and during this acute mental crisis he persuades himself that it is his duty to surrender Haldin to the authorities as represented by General T—— and Councillor Mikulin. His betrayal of the guilty man to death does not, however, enable Razumov to regain the personal freedom he desires; for hereafter, suspected by the government, he is forced to abandon his studies and to become a tool of Mikulin and the secret police. Mikulin sends him to Geneva for the purpose of informing upon a group of Russian conspirators with their headquarters at the Chateau Borel; and here his meeting with the mother and sister of Haldin, who assume that he has been a close friend of the dead man, adds further misery to the doubly false role that has been thrust upon him. Before yielding, however, to the temptation to draw Haldin's sister, Natalia, into the web of evil which surrounds him, Razumov casts off the burden of deceit by an open confession of his guilt to the horrified girl who loves him and to the enraged conspirators who cripple him in revenge.

The curious relationship, at times suggesting a divided personality, between the two young men, the active Haldin and the intellectual Razumov, is strongly reminiscent of tales like "Il Conde," "The Duel," and "The Secret Sharer" which also deal with the sudden and unexpected association of two characters, one of whom is the antithesis or even adversary of the other. Haldin resembles Leggatt in that he is a strong and determined youth who comes secretly and in the shadow of a crime to surprise another man and to endanger his life with a request for help. But even more plainly than Leggatt, Haldin serves, among other things, as a measure of the limitations of ordinary human nature in Razumov, very much as MacWhirr does in respect to Jukes in *Typhoon.* Haldin also makes heroic and impossible claims upon frail mortality, and Conrad treats him as ambivalently as he does MacWhirr.

The portrayal of Haldin as a combination of the admirable and the absurd is another example of Conrad's procedure when dealing with characters who, in seeking to realize an ideal in a world of error, ultimately cause more evil than good. Haldin's prototypes are, therefore, men like Lingard, Jim, and Gould—all of them utopian dreamers. The comparison with Gould seems particularly apt, however, since Haldin is likewise thoroughly sincere in his desire to cleanse a corrupt social order and so ardent in his belief in justice as to exercise in his own person the high function of judge and the lower office of the assassin. Yet just as Gould betrays his own ideal through the human weakness of his impulse to reopen the mine, so also Haldin by obeying his impulse to seek refuge with Razumov precipitates that sequence of events started by human folly which Razumov, in contemplating his own disaster, regards as unchangeable:

> He stared in dreary astonishment at the absurdity of his position. He thought with a sort of dry, unemotional melancholy; three years of good work gone, the course of forty more perhaps jeopardized—turned from hope to terror, because events started by human folly link themselves into a sequence which no sagacity can foresee and no courage can break through.
>
> (XXII, 83)

Haldin aids unknowingly, therefore, in the crushing of Razumov by the same relentless logic of unreason that sweeps the Verlocs to their death. Honest though he is, Haldin is an enthusiast who sees no possibilities of error in himself; and perhaps without realizing the part that he has chosen, he adopts the behavior of Messiah, of Savior, of the human-divine.

Irony at Haldin's assumption of a Christlike role in a world of chance runs throughout the novel. His mother, for example, thinks of him constantly as a leader of apostles among whom there may be a Judas (XXII, 115). And she is, in fact, right; for he finds his disciple and at the same time his Judas in Razumov, who is forced into this position by circumstance rather than conviction. As a prophet of individual redemption through violence, Haldin compels the solitary Razumov to seek redemption indeed, not as a way into a better life, but merely as a relief from fallen man's old plight of sin and its consequences. He gains salvation like a prisoner who leaps to his death in order to escape the rack. Yet one of the sorriest aspects of this bleak drama is that Haldin cannot be blamed for any impurity in conscious motive; for he, as much as Razumov, falls victim to a corrupt society. Like his sister he has lived devoted to the noblest ideals of courage, faith, patriotism, and liberty; but these are cramped by the fanatical impulse provoked in him by oppression. Conrad lays emphasis on this point in his Author's Note, when he says:

> The ferocity and imbecility of an autocratic rule rejecting all legality and in fact basing itself upon complete moral anarchism provokes the no less imbecile and atrocious answer of a purely Utopian revolutionism encompassing destruction by the first means to hand, in the strange conviction that a fundamental change of hearts must follow the downfall of any given human institutions.
>
> (XXII, x)

Conrad portrays the Russian governmental system as thoroughly vicious. The officials in *The Secret Agent* are not admirable, but they are not openly cynical and spiritually moribund like such bureaucratic automatons as General T—— and Mikulin. Despotism of this order blunts the virtues of the ardent Haldin. His practical aim miscarries;

and the proof of the ultimate degradation of a revolutionary ideal when used to mask personal ambition is the evil milieu of the Chateau Borel, itself no more than the counterpart of the established autocracy. Unlike the gang at the Chateau or the anarchists in *The Secret Agent*, Haldin pursues a selfless aim, but he does not foresee its end in evils beyond his control.

To a great extent, therefore, the Russian environment determines the tragedy of both Haldin and Razumov in advance of their encounter. The dilemma created at the outset for Razumov by Haldin's appearance in his room is almost identically that which Leggatt sets before the Captain in "The Secret Sharer": a choice between the exercise of pity towards a criminal according to the existing legal code, or adherence to that code—safety at the price of betrayal. Like the Captain, Razumov is a youth at the beginning of his life-work, alone and encircled by a sea of human error. Not only his own need but also the absence of all respect for life in a tyrannical regime sharpens his instinct of self-preservation. As he hardens in his resolve to betray Haldin, he does consider for a moment the possible claims upon him of a moral bond between individuals; but although this thought is the first anticipation of the spiritual agony in store for him, it is dulled and then swept away by the terror which now has full control of his reason:

> "Betray. A great word. What is betrayal? They talk of a man betraying his country, his friends, his sweetheart. There must be a moral bond first. All a man can betray is his conscience. And how is my conscience engaged here; by what bond of common faith, of common conviction, am I obliged to

let that fanatical idiot drag me down with him? On the contrary—every obligation of true courage is the other way."

(XXII, 37–38)

The question here is like an echo to that raised by Marlow with reference to Jim's collapse on the *Patna;* for again the problem is how a bond to preserve life can withstand the counterclaims of fear and self-preservation that drive Razumov, like Jim, to betrayal with a display on his part of accurate reasoning based on false emotional premises. The development of the rest of the novel provides the answer to this question. The truth, discovered too late by Razumov at Geneva, is that the bond cannot be denied except at the cost of individual grief; and implied in this knowledge, as in the whole meaning of *The Secret Agent*, is the fact that a society which ignores the moral imperative of this bond destroys itself. In this way *Under Western Eyes* demonstrates the full outcome of that betrayal of human feeling which D'Hubert in "The Duel" and the Captain in "The Secret Sharer" were strong enough to prevent or fortunate enough to avoid.

In his immature intellectual self-confidence, which forms a parallel to Haldin's belief in his own power in action, Razumov shows ignorance of that part of his nature which may overwhelm and misdirect the mind. He suffers from much the same disunity between intellect and instinct as the characters in "The Informer" and "Il Conde"; and his sudden belief at the most extreme point of his crisis of fear in a man who will be "strong and one" (XXII, 33) and who will come at the appointed time as "the great autocrat of the future" (XXII, 35) seems the distorted reflection of his own inner craving for unity as it is also a shrewd intuition on Conrad's part of the grounds for an intellectual's secret respect for power. How contemptible this dream of autocracy becomes when realized is proven to Razumov through his association with Peter Ivanovitch, the head conspirator at the Chateau Borel.

The importance of the bond between individuals is emphasized by the fact that Haldin, in possessing the qualities of courage and strength that Razumov lacks, is in many ways the complement of the man who betrays him, so that even after he has disposed of this "lithe and martial" figure (XXII, 14) Razumov cannot free himself of his presence. In the opening section of the novel, Haldin, who is seen largely through the eyes of his betrayer, appears shadowy, less substantial than the ghost walked over by Razumov in his hallucination of having trodden down his fear (XXII, 55). To bury this phantom with its plea for assistance becomes comparatively easy for Razumov once he has thrown himself into the hands of authority. But one of the most powerful effects in the story is the gradual reassertion and triumph of the principle of a human bond through his acceptance of Haldin as a real and concrete being. Very much as Stevie turns up as an avenger in the person of Winnie in *The Secret Agent*, the lost Haldin returns to confront Razumov through Natalia. All that Razumov has failed to recognize in the living Haldin becomes an immediate influence upon him in the dead man's sister with her strong vitality and beauty (XXII, 102), her capacity to inspire love simply by force of what she is. In the remarkable scene in the glaring, boxlike anteroom of her house where he admits his guilt, the power which draws the confession from him is not that of abstraction but of life, the harmony of the girl's whole nature. In what amounts to a recurrence of the earlier episode between the two men Natalia now stands in her brother's place, and Razumov's eyes open at last to the full significance of a binding faith:

> He raised his face, pale, full of unexpressed suffering. But that look in his eyes of dull, absent obstinacy, which struck and surprised everybody he was talking to, began to pass away. It was as though he were coming to himself in the awakened consciousness of that marvellous harmony of feature, of lines, of glances, of voice, which made of the girl before him a being so rare, outside, and, as it were, above the common notion of beauty.
>
> (XXII, 342–43)

This knowledge of the transcendency of personal values is the only reward obtained by Razumov for the loss of all his hopes in his servitude to a cause in which he does not believe. The recompense is, after all, barren; for his escape from the Chateau Borel gives him only a cripple's freedom to die and the memory of having destroyed Natalia's trust in him. It is of the very essence of this strongly inverted tragedy that Razumov should experience love not as a healing but as a severing power, for his admission of guilt removes the possibility of normal union and makes his isolation more complete even than at the beginning of the story. The circle of human folly closes with Natalia's exposure to the evil which has warped Razumov's life. None of the main characters escape the net of circumstance that the well-meaning Haldin has helped to spread. Just as Gould's utopian vision of freedom and justice ends in the paradise of snakes at the silver mine, so also Haldin's vague scheme to bring a new revelation of liberty to birth in Russia comes to earth in the "terroristic wilderness" and in "the apes of the sinister jungle" (XXII, ix) of the Chateau Borel. The desolate Razumov, sitting with bowed head under the bronze effigy of Rousseau (XXII, 291), bears the brunt of another utopian venture.

One of the novel's most memorable episodes, made visually concrete by a tableau of carefully posed and lighted figures (XXII, 327–28), occurs when the narrator, the old English teacher of languages, interrupts a secret meeting of the Chateau Borel plotters in the upper room of a Genevan hotel. On a table at the center lies a colored map of Russia brilliantly illuminated by a shaded electric bulb; and in the arc of shadow beyond, the conspirators stand motionless around their leader, Peter Ivanovitch, who in dark glasses and dressing gown resembles a monk or prophet, "something Asiatic" (XXII, 329). This grouping suggests to the narrator a military conspiracy in Russia; and as he leaves, he reflects that settled Europe has been given in his person "something like a glimpse behind the scenes" (XXII, 330).

Although this remark by a character chosen to embody a Western point of view does express Conrad's antipathy to Russia and his contempt for autocracy,[13] the novel itself, while aimed at demonstrating Russian psychology, is not too far removed from the general conceptual frame surrounding *Nostromo* and *The Secret Agent*. In moving from a story of

13. For statements by Conrad on Russia and Russian autocracy see the essays "Autocracy and War," "The Crime of Partition," and "A Note on the Polish Problem," in Vol. III: *Notes on Life and Letters.*

capitalistic enterprise in South America on to one dealing with London society at different levels and finally to a novel with a background of two of the great cities in Russia and central Europe, Conrad completed a body of work which rewards abundantly a long and close study of his vision of European civilization in his time. Because of their rich content and complicated organization, these books hold more for the reader than any brief critical analysis can indicate; yet an attempt to compare them on the basis of a few common features may be useful in showing that, like the writings of the earlier phase, they reveal an underlying unity of outlook. As the problem that takes form in Conrad's first stories may be defined briefly as the survival of man as a complete human being in a universe without perceptible order, that of the middle stage is in broadest terms man's position in a society increasingly menaced by outbreaks of unreason and violence. In this respect *Under Western Eyes*, allowing for its unique place in the whole of Conrad's fiction, may be regarded as a grim statement of an attitude present in the other novels. Cruel and insane as life appears through all of the ironies of *The Secret Agent*, it is not quite the dead end of hopes and desires that it becomes in *Under Western Eyes;* and Conrad seems to have found in the Russia of his day the most appropriate stage for a drama that would convey to the British reader his darkest premonition of the growing danger of irrationality. The "glimpse behind the scenes" obtained by the language teacher in the hotel room is, no doubt, a flash of political insight; but it is also reminiscent of the glimpses of evil under the apparently ordered surface of life permitted to characters like Marlow and Winnie Verloc.

And the figure of Peter Ivanovitch, upon whom the narrator's glance lingers, although it personifies autocracy and greed for power, is likewise an Asiatic and hence more ominous symbol of the moral insanity of Mr. X in "The Informer" and of the Professor in *The Secret Agent*.

Since Conrad fixed his attention primarily upon moral and psychological weakness in man and in society, he should not, perhaps, be called a political novelist except in the most general sense. As critics have pointed out and as his letters often show, Conrad's political interests, backed by a wide reading of history, were neither superficial nor narrow.[14] His stories display an accurate comprehension of the larger operations of public affairs and movements and, even more significantly, of the influence of social instability and tension upon the private or inner life of the individual. But they have little to do with the play of current political theories or ideas that may be found in the work of Meredith or Shaw or, at a later time, of Rex Warner. Although he had the ordinary man's objection to despotic government, Conrad seems to have been sceptical of institutions as having it in their means to contribute in any way to the good of mankind.[15] But he was equally critical, as may be seen especially in *Nostromo*, of violent change; and the one political phenomenon that roused him to opposition and that stimulated him creatively

14. See R. L. Mégroz, *Joseph Conrad's Mind and Method*, p. 130.

15. In his essay, "Anatole France," Conrad attributes the following political judgment to the French writer: "He is indulgent to the weaknesses of the people, and perceives that political institutions, whether contrived by the wisdom of the few or the ignorance of the many, are incapable of securing the happiness of mankind."—III: *Notes on Life and Letters*, 33.

was revolution, which, in his stories at least, is usually connected with the use of explosives and the infliction of cruelty and death.[16] Conrad disliked revolutionists not because of any hard-grained conservatism on his part but because it seemed to him that they advanced a claim to "special righteousness" which, with his distinctly guarded opinion of human strength and wisdom, he was unwilling to concede. Even the most pardonable revolutionaries in his tales, like Haldin, have this trait of righteousness and of special calling which leads them to forget their limited place in a fallen world.

Despite, therefore, his satiric portrayal of officials like the Monteros and Sotillo in *Nostromo*, General T——— and Mikulin in *Under Western Eyes*, and the Minister of State in *The Secret Agent*, Conrad cares less about the state in itself as a background for his stories than about man as an individual. But he is concerned with order, or better its disappearance, in the society to which man belongs; and true order depends, finally, upon the existence of human bonds. When relationships of this kind fail or when society no longer heeds them, the individual suffers through division and betrayal. Conrad begins at this time, and the interest carries over into his later work, to bring love between man

16. The following statement by Conrad helps to illuminate his portrayal of revolutionaries: "The revolutionary spirit is mighty convenient in this, that it frees one from all scruples as regards ideas. Its hard, absolute optimism is repulsive to my mind by the menace of fanaticism and intolerance it contains.... All claim to special righteousness awakens in me that scorn and anger from which the philosophical mind should be free...."—VI: *A Personal Record*, xxi–xxii.

and woman into the foreground and to stress the consequences of its neglect through a decline of moral feeling in society; for as its character is defensive rather than aggressive and because it safeguards life, love gives evidence of man's acceptance of his limitations and of his willingness to establish a protective bond with another of his kind.

Without such human ties nothing stands in the way of that train of fatal events leading to the supremacy of death over love which is one of the main features of interest in Conrad's work at this stage. Each of the novels begins with a deed incapable of rational explanation, and out of this act proceeds a sequence of evils which destroy the lives of guilty and innocent impartially. Like the bond that should hold it in check, this chain of fatality is also the product, from the negative side, of man's limited nature; for it originates through ignorance or acceptance of the irrational in human motives when the individual displays unwarranted confidence in his own powers. The characters responsible for the initial act—Gould, Vladimir, Haldin—are all men thoroughly self-assured with regard to their intellect or their ideals; and perhaps Conrad's most notable insight into the modern temperament, exhibited with special force in Gould, is his grasp of the paradoxical association of intellectual and imaginative strength with irrational weakness. The familiar division of mind from instinct appears again as a major flaw in character and as a cause for social insecurity. Conrad recognized that with all of his culture, his legal codes, his ponderous administrative machines, modern man lacks adequate defense against "the logic of unreason" and the simple will to die rather than live. For this reason the connoisseur dines with the apostle of destruction in "The Informer," the Count permits the braggart to frighten him to death in "Il Conde," and the Professor laughs in the faces of all the guardians of the state in *The Secret Agent.* The reader today is not likely to overlook Conrad's attention to this point.

Possibly as a contrast to the man of divided nature, Conrad cherished an image of "a man strong and one"—not, however, the future autocrat of Razumov's crooked fancy but an individual capable of self-mastery and hence not prone to sacrifice himself to error and the irrational. In his own experience he had met the living model for such a type in the Mediterranean seaman, Dominic Cervoni, whom Conrad eulogizes in *The Mirror of the Sea* (1906) as "doubly initiated into the most awful mysteries" and whom he places side by side with Ulysses himself:

> And Dominic Cervoni takes his place in my memory by the side of the legendary wanderer on the sea of marvels and terrors, by the side of the fatal and impious adventurer, to whom the evoked shade of the soothsayer predicted a journey inland with an oar on his shoulder, till he met men who had never set eyes on ships and oars.
>
> (IV, 183)

That Conrad held initiation into the mysteries of an irrational world valuable in acquiring self-knowledge of human limits may be seen in stories like "The Duel" and "The Secret Sharer." Despite the pressure of convention or of circumstance the heroes of these tales survive their ordeal by opposing self-betrayal and adhering to a human bond. In the final phase of his creative work Conrad proved that the possibilities of these themes were by no means exhausted, for he introduced them again into stories with some remarkable changes in manner and content.

Chapter 4

THE KNIGHT

Man in Eden

IF the work of Conrad's middle period is heavily charged with tragic irony, that of his final years often has a tragicomic flavor that recalls the mood of *Typhoon* and "Falk" and suggests the ultimate refinement of a talent natural to him from the beginning.[1] This note of comic irony, evident not so much in the material itself as in Conrad's attitude to his subject and in the voice that speaks in the narrative, seems to reflect a growing spirit of confidence in the writer. An essential sanity of outlook penetrates the veil of darkness and morbidity falling upon so many of the stories in this phase and prevails at the end in the cry of "steady" and the brave flutter of the tricolor above the sea where Peyrol of *The Rover* goes down with the tartane. Increasing success with the public may partly explain signs of creative relaxation in Conrad at this time; but the change in tone, like

1. The first short story that Conrad is known to have written, "The Black Mate" (in *Tales of Hearsay*, 1925), is partly comic.

that which came with *Nostromo*, is best accounted for by changing inspiration and not by declining energy. Although there are weak stories in his later work, some of these are experimental and presage genuine achievement with similar materials; and where he is successful, it is plainly evident that Conrad has moved on to explore a new field of irony and to develop what is perhaps his most characteristic theme—the fall of the knightly rescuer. There are indications, particularly in the long-delayed novel of *The Rescue*, that Conrad had been working toward a suitable manner of expressing this theme from early in his career; and for this reason it is in the stories of the last phase that the reader finds the main thematic structure of Conrad's work completed.

The ship of Conrad's success came home, nevertheless, with a strangely assorted cargo, all of it roped by a hand familiar with the most intricate knots. But the smooth, at times almost slick, finish of the later tales does not conceal in them a kind of literary contraband—a small store of absinthe tucked away with the best of marketable goods. *Chance*, his first novel to prove financially rewarding, is, for all of its exciting plot and blandly happy ending, a story which holds the reader in suspense over an affair of delayed consummation managed with all of a courtesan's finesse. And although *Chance* is not the representative book of Conrad's last period, it has in common with many of the rest a heroine, Flora de Barral, who fits the definition of what Mr. Mario Praz has called "the persecuted maiden." [2] The same type of victim of the world's cruelty, at once childish and seductive, can be found again in Alice Jacobus in "A Smile of Fortune," Lena

2. Mario Praz, *The Romantic Agony*, p. 95 and Chapter III *passim*.

in *Victory*, Arlette in *The Rover*, and even in the glamorous Rita—or one of the Ritas—of *The Arrow of Gold*.

By contrast to these damsels in distress one finds in other stories women vain and often spiritually empty—like Freya in "Freya of the Seven Isles," Felicia Moorsom in "The Planter of Malata," and Edith Travers in *The Rescue*—who, though endowed with more robust physical charm than the mistreated heroines, have a similar capacity to stimulate a perverse fascination, to dispense a love potion conforming to Wagnerian recipe. These enchantresses are wholly different from the few who appear in Conrad's earlier tales, like the Aïssa of *An Outcast* who, by comparison with the actress playing this role in Mr. Carol Reed's interesting movie version of the novel, hardly seems more than a wraith. The presence of these women enlarges in Conrad's art an erotic strain of little importance before this time but a not altogether unexpected development from the love motif in the middle novels. The treatment of love between man and woman, a matter of central concern in the last stories, is, however, a new feature in Conrad's writing and one that relates immediately to his firmest convictions.

To complement this group of distressed and distressing heroines, Conrad provides an array of men of knightly appearance and lofty intention, like Anthony in *Chance*, Heyst in *Victory*, Renouard in "The Planter of Malata," and Lingard in *The Rescue*. What distinguishes all of these heroes is their readiness to assume the role of rescuer or savior, and in accordance with chivalric tradition their aim is the rescue of a persecuted maiden or a lady whom they think it necessary to save. But although they are admirable for high qualities of idealism in the abstract, they find their vows troublesome in practice; for their ideals and visions are inspired by a heightened sensuality which Baudelaire would have understood far better than Galahad. Their quest ends in disaster or near disaster for the reason that their attempt at salvation of woman as a human being is confused with their pursuit of a phantasmal Aphrodite.

The figure of the rescuer deceived by illusion becomes, therefore, as prominent in Conrad's later work as the hermit in his earlier; and there is, in fact, an essential resemblance between these types in that they are both deviations from the norm of limited man. Conrad had portrayed chivalrous men—among them Jim, Whalley, and Gould—almost from the first; but they met defeat not through erotic weakness but by the larger force of the irrational in the life about them or in the unconscious side of their own natures. Yet the relationship between these fallen idealists and the erring knights can be traced to their common failure to overcome a division between mind and instinct. The knight deluded by a false vision of the senses thus provides a new image of a defect in the modern temperament on the side of sexual love to succeed that of the anchorite detached from action or withdrawn from a communal bond. Mortal danger attacks the knight, moreover, as it does the hermit, not from outside foes but from an internal enemy, a satanic counterpart of the idealized self, who makes his appearance in moments of crisis. The point of Conrad's ironical and allegorical method in the final phase is clarified for the reader by the fact that the rescuers are squired by grotesque shapes of evil, men like Heemskirk in "Freya," De Barral in *Chance*, Jones and his gang in *Victory*, and Ortega in *The Arrow of Gold*. Although Conrad had experimented frequently with this kind of doubling device for an ironical purpose throughout his career, it was not until the last stories with their more obvious allegorical patterns that its function could be demonstrated in a conclusive way.

The following discussion may help to show that the knight is in certain respects an even more potent figure of irony than the hermit; for the pseudochivalric temper, in which Christian and primitive modes of sexual feeling become fused in erotomysticism, renders itself absurd in a fashion that the solitary need not display. A spirit of ridicule can be discerned in Conrad's handling of mock asceticism in his earlier stories; but the mordant portrayal in *Under Western Eyes* of Peter Ivanovitch, who presides over the sinister temple of the Chateau Borel as a high priest of the cults of revolution and of woman, foreshadows some of the heavier strokes of irony that fall in the later work. A faith built upon the cultivation of sense leads to visions of an artificial paradise of erotic desire which inhibit the impulse to the primary creative act in man and woman, their means of resisting evil and death in a fallen world where there is no prospect of an Eden restored. The value of a bond of normal love derives from the fact that life demands fulfillment in a struggle to maintain order against chaos. In contrasting the false chivalric with the genuine in attitudes to love in his finest work at this stage, Conrad made further use of his creational imagery of lost Eden, Fall, and Deluge; but he added for the first time the metaphor of man's triumph over the ancient enemy of the human pair.

Clear traces of Conrad's later manner are evident in the first and the last of the three long tales published in *'Twixt Land and Sea* (1912), a volume that marked the improvement in his fortunes after the unfavorable reception of *Under Western Eyes*.[3] Although the book included a masterpiece in "The Secret Sharer," the companion stories cannot be measured by that standard of accomplishment, despite the fact that they have merits of a different order. The appeal of "A Smile of Fortune" and "Freya" for the general public perhaps lay in exotic setting and the new love interest which Conrad brewed up with a generous dash of spice once he had determined to try his hand at it. Yet these tales, read attentively, have in them much less sweet than acid; for the erotic element, which is everywhere permeated by a cunning tissue of insinuation, fades out with the rise of the concluding theme of the disillusionment of sensual love. For the reader interested in Conrad's whole development, much of the importance of these stories lies in their resemblance in several respects to the first major work of this period, the novel *Chance*, which came soon afterward. They both play, in a less complicated fashion, upon the ideas of chivalric conduct and of delayed consummation, which appear more prominently in *Chance;* and it is possible that they were written while the design of the novel was taking shape in Conrad's mind.

The principal characters in the sardonically named "A Smile of Fortune"—the young Captain whose inexperience and long absence from the land make him easy prey to the enchantment of a kind of Kundry's garden of massed trop-

3. Conrad, XIX: *'Twixt Land and Sea*, vii.

ical flowers; the ship chandler, Jacobus, something of a Klingsor of the commercial world; and his daughter, Alice, the first of Conrad's persecuted maidens—anticipate the trio of Anthony, De Barral, and Flora in *Chance*. At the beginning of his career and with his foot in the stirrup of command (XIX, 88), the Captain behaves like an untried knight eager for adventure as he brings his ship to the island and the dreamlike vision which a sordid bargain will destroy (XIX, 3). His infatuation with the sensuous beauty of Alice, the sullen girl whom her father keeps secluded in the garden of his house as a temptation to seamen with whom he wishes to trade, places him at last in a compromising position and in the power of Jacobus who sells him a useless cargo of potatoes. Before his downfall, however, the Captain contemplates the idea of acting as rescuer to the socially outcast Jacobus father and daughter:

> ...I had a conception of Jacobus and his daughter existing, a lonely pair of castaways, on a desert island; the girl sheltering in the house as if it were a cavern in a cliff, and Jacobus going out to pick up a living for both on the beach—exactly like two shipwrecked people who always hope for some rescuer to bring them back at last into touch with the rest of mankind.
>
> (XIX, 39)

Since this rescue never takes place and the Captain misses the opportunity to release Alice from her lonely existence, the issue between ideal and sensual motives is never directly broached, as it is in *Chance*, even though the Captain's failure to break through the erotic spell cast over him by Alice to the girl as a human being in distress leaves this conflict in the background of the tale.

Despite her primitive simplicity Alice Jacobus prepares the way for Flora in *Chance* and for similar types of women in the later stories in that she combines a hysterical fear of life with the physical allurement of a tragic victim. These traits ensnare the Captain and hinder him from action by tempting him to maintain a bond dependent upon irrealizable desire (XIX, 59). Devoid of genuine pity, his longing is for unique sensation alone (XIX, 62); and this quest ends in his knowledge that "it is in seeking the unknown in our sensations that we discover how mediocre are our attempts and how soon defeated!" (XIX, 79–80). After his surrender to the wiles of Jacobus he cannot remember the garden without also the smell of rotting potatoes for a reminder of his loss of a false paradise in a fallen world.

Compared with "A Smile of Fortune," "Freya of the Seven Isles," the last of the tales in this volume, appears at first less vigorous because of a looser plot and a slower rise in the action. Taken literally, this melodramatic story of passion and revenge turns on the whim of Freya, the beautiful but headstrong daughter of a Danish planter, to delay her marriage with Jasper Allen, the owner and master of the brig *Bonito*. Made reckless by the generosity of her lover in his obedience to her wishes, Freya yields to the impulse to humiliate Allen's rival, the Dutch naval officer Heemskirk, who revenges himself by stranding the brig and destroying the hopes of the lovers. Examined closely, however, the story may be seen to conform much more exactly than "A Smile of Fortune," to Conrad's customary method of dealing with a psychological and moral problem. Its pattern corresponds to that of the novels of the second period in that a train of fatal accidents, set off by Freya's resolve to hold Allen's desire in suspense, encounters an abnormal relationship between a man and woman who are not united in resistance. The fairly elaborate machinery of the tale—in particular the use made of the two ships, Allen's brig and Heemskirk's gunboat—belongs to Conrad's familiar practice of employing visual detail rather than analysis and looks forward to the heavy allegorical framework of *The Rescue.*

By an arrangement of realistic materials Conrad cloaked a situation based upon the outcome of arrested sexual passion without venturing so far as he did soon afterwards in *Chance.* In the story there is nothing to compare with Anthony's deliberate vow of chastity, and only by inference from Freya's hysterical behavior after she has sent Allen away on a trading cruise and from the reader's knowledge of the emotions that they are holding in check can the man's reaction to their pact be determined. The scene in which the overwrought Freya taunts Heemskirk with chords of Wagnerian love music from her piano is not pretty; and were it not for the fact that the Dutchman is little more than the puppet of a single appetite, the episode would seem even uglier by reason of Freya's enjoyment of the thrill of being able to attract both Allen's infatuation and Heemskirk's desire (XIX, 204). The emphasis at this point serves, however, to direct the reader's attention to the true significance of Heemskirk, whose swarthiness contrasts so markedly with the fairness of Allen and Freya, as an embodiment of the evil which takes possession of Allen by his humoring of Freya's caprice. Allen's separation from Freya gives Heemskirk his opportunity for revenge.

This situation contains the germ of what will later become the more sinister drama in the cabin of the *Ferndale* in *Chance*, although there the stress will fall upon the perilous division within the man and not, as in the short story, upon the effect of renunciation in the woman. Jasper Allen, whose resemblance to "a flashing sword-blade perpetually leaping out of the scabbard" (XIX, 158) makes him the first of Conrad's knightly characters in this phase to whom such metaphors are applied, is Anthony's predecessor at least in his extremely idealistic attitude towards woman and his capacity for intense emotion. The lofty nature of Allen's idealization of love is projected in the image of the gleaming brig so magnanimously dedicated to Freya. But without the actual presence of the woman the ideal cannot remain indefinitely self-sustaining; and the "finely tempered and trusty sword-blade" breaks in "the common cudgel-play of Fate" (XIX, 167). Like its master, the brig falls captive in the end to the black gunboat of Heemskirk, a craft also haunted by the spirit of Freya (XIX, 211). The theme of erotic abnormality with its excessive demands upon limited human beings thus appears for the first time in full strength.

With an astonishing rise in creative vigor, Conrad transformed the raw substance of unconventional sexual behavior in the two stories just discussed into material adapted to all the refinements of tragicomic ambivalence in *Chance* (1913). This gain in dexterity over the somewhat ponderous handling of the shorter tales owes much to the reintroduction of Marlow as narrator and amateur psychoanalyst; for without his British growl of irony and common sense resounding across the deeps of human perplexity, the novel would probably not have quite that oddness of tone which is part of its distinction. His voice establishes a reassuring front of master mariner's wisdom behind which his creator directs the play with his own nervous hand. Marlow proclaims, and his appearance almost guarantees, the ultimate victory of the normal over the abnormal. But the normal wins by curious tactics, among them a well-timed peep through the cabin skylight of the *Ferndale* in the extraordinary denouement which brings to a climax a line of action poised between the absurd and the tragic.

Strictly in terms of the narrative itself, however, Marlow's principal function is to keep the reader in touch with the psychological and moral implications of this first main venture by Conrad into the field of melodrama, possibly the most successful and mature reworking of this genre in the British novel in the earlier years of this century. The tight design imposed upon *Chance* by knitting up diverse threads of circumstance is in the tradition of Wilkie Collins and Dickens;[4] and the climactic scene in the poisonous atmosphere of the *Ferndale's* saloon, the conventional tightly enclosed melodramatic setting, rivals the best work of those masters for power of invention. But *Chance* is melodrama of the highest order; and the traditional duel between vice and virtue reveals the most secret motives of the human heart,

4. In *A Personal Record* Conrad twice refers to his reading of Dickens. He mentions having read *Nicholas Nickleby*, perhaps in 1870 (VI, 71). He also speaks of *Bleak House* as a work for which he had "an intense and unreasoning affection, dating from the days of my childhood" (VI, 124). In conversations with R. L. Mégroz, Conrad praised Chesterton's book on Dickens and spoke of Dickens himself as "quite a good man; his work is wonderful."—R. L. Mégroz, *Joseph Conrad's Mind and Method*, pp. 21, 36.

particularly in the catastrophe where the happy ending avoids tragedy by the narrowest margin.

The background of *Chance* is the same world of irrationality and error with its coiled spring of destruction as that of *The Secret Agent*, though more realistic and without the latter's single atmospheric tone. The issue once again becomes a question of life or death as evil seeks to penetrate human resistance at its spot of decay. Captain Anthony, who for years has led a bachelor's life as master of the sailing ship *Ferndale*, comes ashore in England to visit his sister and her husband, the Fynes, and while staying with them in the country falls suddenly in love with the youthful Flora de Barral, the daughter of a ruined financier who has been tried and imprisoned for fraud. Flora's exposure to the cruelties of the world after her removal from a sheltered life under her father's protection has left her with a psychic injury and brought her close to suicide; and with mixed feelings of sympathy and passion, Anthony determines to act as rescuer by marrying her and taking her to sea with him. A remark by his brother-in-law, Fyne, to the effect that Anthony is taking advantage of the girl's distress stabs the Captain's pride so that he resolves to prove his magnanimity not only by assigning his wife separate quarters on the ship but also by making room for her father after the latter's discharge from prison. By this arrangement for creating suffering for himself, misunderstanding in Flora, and hatred in De Barral, Anthony, with much of Freya's reckless indifference to mortal weakness, flings "a glove in the face of nature" (II, 351); and in answer to his challenge the dark powers join to press him to the brink of disaster. In the closing chapters, with everyone except the young mate, Powell, in a condition of tortured nerves, the shadows of a darkening universe fall upon the sea (II, 292–93). Doom threatens in the near collision of the *Ferndale* with her cargo of dynamite and another ship (II, 320). The last act in the ship's cabin, when Powell breaks in to save Anthony from De Barral's poison, rises above superb melodrama to universal allegory of the conflict between good and evil, the normal and the abnormal, for the possession of Anthony's soul.

This somber color blends, however, with the comic so as to give *Chance* something of the quality of dark comedy in contrast to the clearly marked tragic line of the novels of Conrad's middle period. This comic note emanates from the central situation created by Anthony, who is the first heroic-absurd figure after Gould in *Nostromo* to equal the latter in chivalric deportment. But whereas the chivalry of Gould dedicates itself to the restoration of justice, that of Anthony concentrates on the salvation of a woman; and in Anthony and Flora, the "Knight" and the "Damsel" of the headings of the two main divisions of the novel, Conrad establishes a relationship well adapted to the purpose of satire on the romantic convention exalted in the poetry written by Anthony's father and applied in reality with such perilous consequences by the son. Anthony's behavior corresponds to the traditional pattern of the amatory tales of knighthood much more obviously than that, for example, of the young Captain in "A Smile of Fortune." The inexperienced knight in *Chance* descends into an evil commercial world, rescues "the most forlorn damsel of modern times" (II, 238), and carries her off to the sanctuary of the seaman's order. But the quest, through Anthony's ill-timed vow of renunciation, ends not in freedom but in captivity; and the rescuer himself has to be saved by a youth with a simple eye for fact. In itself the redemption of the damsel is a fine gesture, but neither the motives for it nor the act of denial which completes it are altogether consonant with the ideals of the Table Round or Monsalvat; and Anthony, as Marlow says, forgets that there are limits to human undertakings:

> "... the magnanimous Anthony had carried off his conquest and—well—his self-conquest too, trying to act at the same time like a beast of prey, a pure spirit and the 'most generous of men.' Too big an order clearly because he was nothing of a monster but just a common mortal, a little more self-willed and self-confident than most, maybe, both in his roughness and in his delicacy."
>
> (II, 415–16)

Yet even though Anthony reveals his kinship with common humanity by his limited capacity for moral endurance, he is still the son of a delicately erotic poet (II, 309) who has sung in praise of "highly civilized, chivalrous love" (II, 332); and in the solitude of his seafaring existence the Captain appears to have developed a refined sensitivity not only to the spirit of his father's verse but also to aesthetic impressions inspired by Flora's beauty, a beauty which she has acquired through her ill-treatment by the world. In passing from Alice Jacobus to Flora, Conrad subtilized his handling of the persecuted-maiden theme to a marked degree; for although both of these women are outcast victims and haunted by fear, the voluptuous charm of Alice looks hearty beside the pallor of Flora with its suggestion of that tragic sorrow in

Pater's definition of modern beauty (II, 217). A terrifying revelation to her in adolescence of the passions of avarice and sexual jealousy in a mature woman, her governess, leaves the "mystic wound" on Flora's soul (II, 118); and the irony of her story is that this stigma should hasten the flowering of the beauty shadowed by death that first lays upon Anthony the great and fatal love spell and then becomes a factor in his generous deed which is even more cruel than the malice of the governess.

Anthony's passion for Flora grows out of complicated roots in morbidity, violence, and profound sympathy; and the swift wave of his desire holds this balance safely until his assumption of a chivalrous pose checks the impulse. Conrad's study of Anthony is perceptive in its recognition that erotic and ideal motives are in certain temperaments so indistinguishable that one may be the outgrowth of the other and that pity so far from being pure only when removed from the influence of sexual feeling, as a Schopenhauerian might contend and as Anthony tries to demonstrate, loses its dross of contempt when love works as the refining agent. Anthony's passion is sincere enough to transcend the sensual, predatory, and even rapacious appetites that helped to kindle it (II, 223–24). It is, nevertheless, the expression of a nature more given to extremes than the average; hence it bears within it that vein of evil which Flora, immature in years but already initiated into the most savage emotions by the governess, detects in the flash of her thought that Anthony might strangle her in a fury of disappointment (II, 229). Fyne's remark that Anthony's kindness to Flora is really a "pitiless transaction" helps to quicken this evil.

Anthony has been "hermit-like" in the earlier course of his life (II, 223); and when he takes command of his ship, fixed in his resolve to answer Fyne's accusation by the magnanimous gesture which turns Flora to stone in the belief that Anthony does not love her (II, 335), he ceases to be the knightly man of action and becomes instead, by immuring himself in his cabin, a hermit like those in Conrad's earliest stories. In attempting to reconcile his idealism and his instincts, he falls helpless before the intrusion of evil; and in order to dramatize this struggle of a divided soul without resorting to analysis, Conrad sets in motion one of his most successful vehicles of psychological allegory. From the opening of the second half of the novel where the setting changes from land to sea, all of the action points toward the final stage for this drama, the *Ferndale's* saloon with its symbolic curtain that separates Anthony from his fellow officers —the same curtain image which Conrad had used as early as *Almayer's Folly* [5] and that he will use again to excellent effect in *Victory*—and its peculiar floor plan which interests Marlow because of its "moral atmosphere" (II, 415), that sinister atmosphere which Conrad imparts with mastery to all of his questionable interiors from Hervey's mansion in "The Return" to the house in the street of the Consuls in *The Arrow of Gold*. Since Anthony and Flora have become passive as a result of the barrier between them, the lead in this allegorical drama falls to Powell and De Barral.

Conrad drew his villains black, not primarily for melodramatic effect but because he intended them to embody moral evil so plainly that they could be distinguished from

5. Conrad, XI: *Almayer's Folly*, 44, 198, *et passim.*

the fully human characters in his later tales. Although De Barral is less one-dimensional than Heemskirk in "Freya," he comes from the same bag of grotesques; and his function in the allegory is never in doubt from the moment when Powell, going to the poop of the *Ferndale* and catching his first sight of De Barral, takes the latter for Anthony's double:

"In fact, he had no occasion to go on the poop or even look that way much; but while the ship was about to anchor, casting his eyes in that direction, he received an absurd impression that his captain (he was up there, of course) was sitting on both sides of the aftermost skylight at once. He was too occupied to reflect on this curious delusion, this phenomenon of seeing double as though he had had a drop too much."

(II, 276)

Because of Anthony's divided state, the *Ferndale* does, in fact, put to sea with two captains aboard; and the second of these is a fixed idea masquerading as an old man who has gone mad in prison. Haunted by the "lurid visions" of a solitary (II, 362), De Barral doesn't want sacrifice but the life that has been stolen from him (II, 294). He wants neither pity nor generosity but Flora herself (II, 380), and this fixed idea ends in his attempt to murder Anthony. De Barral's favorite seat on deck is the cabin skylight directly above Anthony's head, so that the old man's crazed mutterings give expression to the silent torments of his son-in-law caged below in the saloon with the tyrannical and mortal passion which has invaded him completely (II, 329).

Since Anthony, who is now afflicted as grievously as Flaubert's anchorite of the same name, cannot heal himself, his salvation must come from the "secret watcher" (II, 416), Powell, who is undergoing his initiation into evil as a dedicated servant of the temple of the seafaring order to which Anthony remains attached from the best side of his nature (II, 32). It is, significantly enough, poison, a thing that harms internally, that De Barral pours into Anthony's glass; and Powell's intervention saves the Captain, and Flora as well, from a *crime passionel* in which De Barral would have been merely the accessory rather than the principal. What effect the poison might have had upon Anthony is indicated obliquely by the likeness, mentioned suddenly at the height of the scene in the cabin, between Anthony and Othello and Flora and Desdemona, Anthony appearing "swarthy as an African, by the side of Flora whiter than the lilies" (II, 427). Powell flings back the dividing curtains just in time to save Anthony from Othello's fate and from the triumph of that violence which Flora, in the hour of her wooing, had glimpsed at the heart of her lover's passion. This restoration of the normal brings with it a fulfillment of life's purpose in that "pairing off" which is "the fate of mankind" (II, 426). The reuniting of the human pair places the head of the serpent, De Barral, under the heel of the man, Anthony (II, 433); for it is within Anthony alone that the strife between the normal and the perverse has been waged.

In attempting by his false chivalry to make himself something more, or at least something other, than the ordinary human being that he is under all of his temperamental eccentricities, Anthony degenerates into something less than human and comes near to ending a tool of the powers of darkness. The whole ingenious structure of the allegory at the conclusion of *Chance*, which provides the book with a whole level of meaning over and above the narrative itself, thus stands upon a cardinal point in Conrad's thinking. Anthony's resolution to carry delicacy to a ludicrous extreme is not the asceticism of profound conviction but a course prompted by vanity which forces him into an attitude of negation not unlike that of a disciple of Schopenhauer or of Otto Weininger. In *Chance*, therefore, Conrad's irony exposes the absurdities and perils of a theory of detachment with reference to a special situation and unusual characters. He was to go farther in *Victory* (1915) and to deal in even bolder allegorical terms with the consequences of this doctrine.

The rising action in both *Chance* and *Victory* begins with the rescue of a damsel in distress. Although Lena is a hardier spirit than Flora de Barral, she is also a lonely victim of the world's injustice when Axel Heyst, after his other gestures of a chivalrous kind, offers her salvation from Zangiacomo's traveling band of women in the solitude of his island of Samburan. Both novels have, furthermore, a similar tragicomic note—broken more abruptly in *Victory* by the tragedy of the denouement—and the same conclusion in dramatic allegory with a man helpless before the powers of evil. But whereas the interest in *Chance* is largely psychological, that in *Victory* is as near the philosophical as Conrad ever comes; and his familiar theme of detachment and action takes greater prominence in the later than in the earlier book. The allegory in *Victory* has wider universal significance than the single conflict of good and evil in the individual, for which reason the background myth of lost Eden is more clearly defined than in any other work after *An Outcast*. The story has, moreover, stronger undertones of warning and premonition than *Chance;* and since is was finished in May, 1914,[6] it is perhaps not accidental that the thunder over the closing scene has the sound of a naval action on the horizon (xv, 389).

This sense of imminent disaster, of a world to be swamped by deluge and scoured by fire, that is produced by the cosmic imagery of the conclusion gives an added dimension to Conrad's leading subject of the alliance of the human pair against evil. The firmament darkens in *Chance* as Anthony moves nearer to his hour of trial; but the sky is not torn, as in *Victory*, by a crimson wound like a portent of chaos (xv, 355). Nor, with Powell at hand, are Anthony and Flora so completely dependent upon themselves as Heyst and Lena on the island stagnating in the center of its void of silence. Heyst displays, in addition, more broadly representative traits of modern feeling than Anthony. His prophetic description of himself as "a man of the last hour" or of "the hour before the last" seems hardly applicable to the hero of *Chance* who does not think of belonging to a falling world (xv, 359). The malady of Heyst is a modern low fever of ingrained scepticism. Instinctively he is as readily disposed to action as Anthony, and for this reason his philosophy of detachment is quite as artificial. But thanks to the early influence of his father's belief in a spectatorial attitude to life and to a persistent habit of thought, he can no longer act without self-contempt. This melancholy distrust of existence makes him ineffectual and pathetic, even a little boyish, as Anthony never is; but his more delicate egotism absorbs him and fos-

6. Conrad, XV: *Victory*, vii.

ters a condition of spiritual pride which defies fate more arrogantly than Anthony's masculine vanity.

Because of the inconsistency between his theory of detachment and his active impulses, Heyst assumes a role poised between wider extremes of the ludicrous and the tragic than those present in Anthony. In his resemblance to the adventurous Charles XII (xv, 9), in his martial face, broad shoulders, and "horizontal bar" moustache (xv, 53)—all knightly traits that seem a little out of character in his meditative disposition—he is a somewhat absurd hero; and in the course of the novel it is he who shrinks, whereas Lena grows steadily to near heroic size (xv, 252). For *Victory* follows Biblical tradition in permitting woman to fulfill the task of crushing the serpent's head. Like *Chance*, *Victory* ends with the defeat of the abnormal by the normal in Lena; and in the gravity of this issue the heroism that matters is that enlisted firmly on the side of life—a readiness like that of Powell with his simple vision of fact and of Lena with her passionate will to sacrifice.

Heyst's blindness to the alternatives of life and death explains the presence of the absurd and the pathetic in his character. In mistaking arrogance for delicacy, contempt for pity, he creates a situation wherein the paradoxes of his earlier conduct harden suddenly before the face of evil into a dilemma in which detachment means death and action life. Attacked on the island by Jones, the social outcast, Heyst is compelled to act in order to preserve even the detachment that he has sought for himself and Lena; and when overtaken by the consequences of his negation, he discovers at last, in the abandonment of his godlike pose of spectator of the world's vanities, his humble desire to live. His irresistible temptation to move to the rescue of distressed human beings (xv, 51)—gratified twice in his saving first of Morrison, his partner in the coal venture, and then of Lena—thus becomes in the end productive of more ill than good since the burden of scepticism and of disillusionment smothers the chivalric impulse. Even without its many other features of interest *Victory* would remain, therefore, of singular importance because of the portrayal in Heyst of the clash of an Eastern philosophy of negation with the Western spirit of action. Since he is both knight and hermit, Heyst stands as one of Conrad's most representative characters.

The most telling proof of the inadequacy of the theory of detachment to free Heyst from his bondage to a fallen world is the discovery of his vulnerability through the senses, an element of his nature that he has ignored in practice. This revelation comes in the brilliant comic scene in Schomberg's concert hall—one of the finest examples of Conrad's objective psychological reporting—where Heyst first sees Lena among the members of the women's orchestra. When he enters the hall, the vulgarity of the atmosphere with its garish color—the heat, the smoke, the crimson sashes of the entertainers, the hail of noise from the orchestra (xv, 68)—repels Heyst intellectually; but this violence beating upon his senses stimulates them into preternatural activity so that his tender feelings toward Lena include an undercurrent of sensuality and even potential brutality:

Heyst, quite overcome by the volume of noise, dropped into a chair. In the quick time of that music, in the varied, piercing clamour of the strings, in the movements of the bare arms, in the low dresses, the coarse faces, the stony eyes of the executants, there was a suggestion of brutality—something cruel, sensual and repulsive.

"This is awful!" Heyst murmured to himself. But there is an unholy fascination in systematic noise. He did not flee from it incontinently, as one might have expected him to do.

(xv, 68)

This situation, reminiscent of the elements involved in Anthony's attraction to Flora, introduces again Conrad's theme of the false hermit, his ideals belied by his senses; and Heyst's discovery later on the island that there is a discrepancy between elemental desire and his exalted conception of himself is unfortunate in that it prevents his chivalrous conduct from developing into love. He recognizes that the erotic and chivalric impulses constitute a heresy from the standpoint of his creed of detachment.

The episode in the concert hall followed by the retirement of Heyst and Lena to the island marks the point at which the comic tone of the novel begins to shade gradually into the tragic and where the action moves from the plane of realism to that of allegory. Until this stage the contradictions between Heyst's doctrine of withdrawal and his unexpected sallies into the field of action can be regarded humorously, and the irony in the narrator's voice encourages this reaction. The only forewarnings of the sinister drama to come lie in the failure of the coal enterprise with Morrison and the malice of Schomberg, the hotel keeper who has desired Lena for himself, steps by which Heyst involves himself in the coil of fatality. Were it not for his high regard for scrupulous conduct, the capping of Heyst's inconsistencies by the sealing of a permanent compact with life through woman would be a new version of the tale of the condemner of folly duped himself, the comedy of *Love's Labour's Lost*. But because Heyst, like Anthony, is not a conventional lover, his acceptance of life is a bond formed under duress and fraught, therefore, with misfortune.

Heyst's thought on the island that there is in him a lot of the original Adam provides one of the first clues to the meaning of the remarkable paradisal allegory that crowns the achievement of Conrad in *Victory:*

> Heyst meditated in simple terms on the mystery of his actions; and he answered himself with the honest reflection:
>
> "There must be a lot of the original Adam in me, after all." He reflected, too, with the sense of making a discovery, that this primeval ancestor is not easily suppressed. The oldest voice in the world is just the one that never ceases to speak.
>
> (xv, 174)

Heyst considers the island a refuge from the fates, but it is a fallen Eden threatened by the jungle; and the task of Heyst and Lena is the labor of mortal man and woman to establish a barrier against the inroads of evil. The bridge built of old by the Satanic host from hell to earth touches the jetty on Samburan; and Schomberg revenges himself on Heyst by pointing the way for the ancient enemies of the human pair —evil intelligence, lust, and brute force (xv, 329)—just as Willems in *An Outcast* opens the portals for the entry of the Arabs into Sambir. Jones and his followers, Ricardo and Pedro, divide in their unholy trinity the single force of evil embodied in De Barral in *Chance*, and this division is well adapted to a situation relating much more closely to the

Biblical setting of humanity's conflict with the powers of darkness than the allegory of Anthony's resistance to the morbid promptings of his own nature aboard the *Ferndale*. Like De Barral, Jones and Ricardo have a passion for gambling; but it is the master passion of the world of chance wherein they control the board (xv, 118).

The allegory has also, however, its reference to the soul of man; for the partnership of Jones and Ricardo, those "identical souls in different disguises" (xv, 130), is the true reflection of Heyst's own contempt for life. The repeated assertion by Jones that he and Heyst have something in common is literal truth (xv, 321), just as De Barral proves to be Anthony's double. Jones derives from hell by way of the Yellow Nineties. He is a kind of *fin-de-siècle* Satan who, as Huysmans once pointed out, was a gentleman. He is not only a symbol of rebellious egotism but also a dissipated pursuer of new sensations (xv, 385), and his horror of woman completes itself in Ricardo's lust. In his revolt from the normal he displays the trait of Satanic pride which is essential to the allegory; for as he forces his company upon Heyst, the latter must recognize in the dominant trait of his enemy the same defiance of life that lies back of his own creed of negation and in the savage desire of Ricardo the violence resulting from a denial of the purpose of existence fulfilled through woman. Because of his inability to break through the curtain of scepticism and sensuality barring him from complete union with Lena, Heyst remains defenseless before Jones and Ricardo; and Lena must die to give him strength to tear down the curtain in the end (xv, 404).

Since Heyst cannot forge between himself and Lena the

defensive bond of love, they are compelled to separate like Adam and Eve in the hour before the Fall—Heyst to meet his appointed foe in Jones, Lena hers in Ricardo. But at the same time, and in accordance with the story of the Fall in its modern application, the forces of evil split and lose the singleness of aim that inspired the original Satan. In his refusal to repress any longer the "soul of savagery," which must break free to kill or ravish (xv, 288), Ricardo disobeys Jones, his "governor"; this disobedience goes far beyond the expression of sensuality that accompanied the Fall in its first manifestation. Ricardo wants blood as a part of the fulfillment of his desire for Lena, and his rift with Jones demonstrates with the same precision that marks the whole of the allegory the impossibility of continuing the partnership of the modern extremes of negation and violence once a rage for destruction causes them to sunder. Woman, whose full significance as a creative figure equally compounded of spirit and sense this alliance of evils denies, stands as the rock upon which this union of opposites must break; and Lena's triumph in depriving Ricardo of his knife is both an assertion of woman's competence to perform her life-task and a rejection of the idea of her subservience to evil. Heyst's terrifying view of the glaring room, where Lena sits enthroned while Ricardo offers the Black Mass of his adoration, brings him final testimony that the doctrine implanted by his father is perverse. He acknowledges the bond of life when the opportunity has been lost; and in the ironical conclusion his Chinese servant, Wang, and a native woman, creatures of instinct, inherit the island (xv, 411).

In *Victory* Conrad achieved the most successful balance

in his later work between realism and allegory, and this helps to explain the continued popularity of the novel. It is also the last of his books in which his ironical talent keeps pace with the development of a theme of general human significance. Hereafter, or at least until *The Rover*, his technical accomplishment seems to exceed at times his facility with narration and character. Books like *The Arrow of Gold* and *The Rescue* show an extreme refinement of his complicated method of visual presentation as well as an extension of his range in social material, since he describes in them levels of modern sophistication that he had touched only in the stories of his middle phase. In these later novels he innovates mainly, however, in transcribing objectively the illusions of sense that figure prominently in *The Arrow of Gold* and importantly again in *The Rescue*. The first clear evidence of his progress in this direction appears in the long opening tale of the *Within the Tides* volume (1915), "The Planter of Malata," which has some resemblances to *Victory* in its island setting but more still to *The Rescue* which it anticipates in the fatal infatuation of the adventurer, Renouard, for the society woman, Felicia Moorsom, so obviously a parallel to Lingard's passion for Edith Travers. Conrad's reference to "The Planter" as "a nearly successful attempt at doing a very difficult thing" is an indication that the story fell short of his intentions; [7] but when read as supplementary to his theme of the defeated knight, the work contains points of interest in its subject matter and in its technical novelties.

The central figure, Geoffrey Renouard, has an even better right than the heroes in the works preceding "The

7. Conrad, X: *Within the Tides*, x.

Planter" to be considered a man of knightly or martial character. By overcoming the hazards of a career of strenuous adventure and exploration (x, 5), he has won control of the island of Malata. But the fate of this "man of definite conquering tasks" (x, 35) is to find himself bound tight in a noose of consequences because he is incapable of withdrawing from an adventure which leads to his own defeat and the desolation of the world that he has created. When the London society beauty, Felicia Moorsom, comes to the South Seas with her father, a philosophy professor, in search of a man who was once her suitor but whom she rejected for his involvement in a financial scandal in England, Renouard falls in love with the young woman after he has promised to help her with her task. Completely dominated by his passion, Renouard conceals from Felicia the fact that the lost man, once Renouard's assistant on Malata, is dead in order that he may enjoy her presence by prolonging the futile search. At the last Renouard confesses to her both his deception and its motive only to learn that she is incapable of passion or concern for anything except her own vanity (x, 77). After her departure he swims out to his death in the sea, so that the final scene, like that in *Victory*, is of an island where the life of white men has ceased to exist.

It seems apparent that in this story, which is heavily symbolic in places, Conrad endeavored to accomplish an ambitious project which would reveal the drift of civilized man away from his foothold "on this earth of passions and death which is not a hothouse" (x, 77). Although Felicia and Renouard are a well-matched couple (x, 50), their love fails because of her insincerity and his inability to resist the sensual infatuation which devitalizes his energy and will. The island, as in *Victory*, lies before man and woman to be governed by their mutual effort; but Felicia renounces this task to devote herself to a cult of the dead man and Renouard to follow the ghost of his assistant into oblivion. In fainter outline the allegory of the human pair in a fallen world can be discerned, therefore, in "The Planter" as well as in *Victory;* but in the shorter tale the characters are nearer to historical types than are those in the novel. Renouard appears, even more than Heyst, symbolic of Western man in his last hour. By calling attention to his resemblance to a bronze figure in a classical museum (x, 75) and to his statuesque profile, Conrad seems to indicate both Renouard's descent from one of the chief sources of Western tradition and also the arrested impulse to action which accompanies his retirement to Malata:

> His face, shaded softly by the broad brim of a planter's panama hat, with the straight line of the nose level with the forehead, the eyes lost in the depth of the setting, and the chin well forward, had such a profile as may be seen amongst the bronzes of classical museums, pure under a crested helmet—recalled vaguely a Minerva's head.
>
> (x, 38)

Renouard's withdrawal to the island is connected with the growing callousness of sentiment that weakens his resistance to sensual stimulation (x, 26), as though Conrad meant here to portray the decline of a faith in action into a cult of sense worship. Almost the first comment about Renouard is that he is a man of active nature (x, 3), but the solitude of Malata so transforms him that the focal point of his being becomes the eye with its abnormally acute visual faculty which fastens upon the brilliant image of Felicia:

> He remembered all this visually, and it was not exactly pleasurable. It was rather startling like the discovery of a new faculty in himself. There are faculties one would rather do without—such, for instance, as seeing through a stone wall or remembering a person with this uncanny vividness.
>
> (x, 12)

In *Victory* Heyst is similarly afflicted with hyperacuity of the senses on his return from isolation in Samburan; but, as the scene in Schomberg's concert hall makes clear, a frenzy affects all of his sensory apparatus and not the eye alone. In considering this aspect of "The Planter," which develops Conrad's theme of vision in a special way, the reader may recall Yeats's concern with the cultural significance of an emphasis upon the eye in painting or sculpture. Some theory of cultural decline appears to underlie "The Planter"; and if it is not one of Conrad's best stories, it certainly does not fail through poverty of content.

By singling out intensity of vision as one cause of Renouard's lapse from the normal, Conrad found means to introduce the vivid yet fantasmal impressions of Felicia under varying conditions of light which constitute the main technical innovation in "The Planter." Until his final experience of her scorn for him Renouard never sees beyond appearance to what Felicia really is. His eye is dazzled by an illusion of an artifact—a creation of precious metals, stones, and ivory cast in a pagan mold (x, 9–10) or a magic painting glowing upon a dark background (x, 47). Unlike Pygmalion's statue, the object of Renouard's devotion can never be touched into life, a truth revealed to him in his dream of pursuing himself and ending by stumbling upon the marble head of a statue with Felicia's face which crumbles in his fingers:

> The sickly white light of dawn showed him the head of a statue. Its marble hair was done in the bold lines of a helmet, on its lips the chisel had left a faint smile, and it resembled Miss Moorsom. While he was staring at it fixedly, the head began to grow light in his fingers, to diminish and crumble to pieces, and at last turned into a handful of dust....
>
> (x, 31)

This interesting example of dream imagery seems to indicate, in the likeness of the helmeted head to Renouard's own classical features, that the woman's form admired by him is in great part a reflection of his own private vision of a sterile Aphrodite. The phantom beauty who holds him enchanted is a forerunner of the exotic Rita of *The Arrow of Gold.*

In its quality of bravura, in its specialized atmosphere of the 1870's in France, and in its partly autobiographical foundation,[8] *The Arrow of Gold* (1919) may at first appear somewhat isolated from the main body of Conrad's work. He himself attributed the note of disappointment in the reviews to the fact that he had produced something unexpected and had essayed a method of presentation which was a new departure in his art.[9] Even today the novel is too frequently set aside by critics as one of the least successful of the later stories,[10] when it is actually one of the most interesting when seen in relation to the main tendencies of his writing at this

8. Conrad, I: *The Arrow of Gold*, viii.
9. G. Jean-Aubry, *Joseph Conrad: Life and Letters,* II, 227, 213.
10. See F. R. Leavis, *The Great Tradition*, p. 182.

time. Under the surface glitter achieved by technical craft alone, the solid lines of the thematic substructure common to all of the work of Conrad's last phase can be discerned—just as, near the close of the book, one seems to have heard from the beginning the approaching footsteps of the crazed Ortega running amok along the back of a forestage shimmering in the light off marble, brocade, and Venetian glass. The action begins with the first encounter of a man accustomed to an isolated life with the suddenly unveiled powers of sense, a formula applied at the opening of "A Smile of Fortune" and afterwards repeated in the varied settings of *Chance*, *Victory*, and "The Planter of Malata." The lady in distress appears again, moreover, in Rita, who bears under her disguise of a modern Gioconda the same psychic wound of fear as Alice Jacobus or Flora de Barral. Her spirit too has been lamed for her first experience with mankind by the scorn poured into her ear as a child still too young to die of fright (I, 96).

Conrad, however, places his familiar theme of damsel and rescuer against a background which he introduces here for the first and last time. The novel is his one attempt to deal with the world of art, or at least with a level of society governed solely by aesthetic standards; and even though the conspiracy to place a Bourbon pretender on the throne of Spain gives an air of adventure to the narrative, the political events take place mainly off stage. In no other book does Conrad work quite so steadily as a painter in prose; and one remembers *The Arrow* as in many respects a gallery of portraits and statues: Rita standing in a blue dress on the crimson carpet of a staircase (I, 66), Therese a figure out of a cracked and smoky painting (I, 138–39), Mrs. Blunt a picture in silver and grey with touches of black (I, 180), and Blunt a marble monument of funereal grace (I, 212). The actors move through a succession of rooms as cluttered with bric-a-brac as those of an antique shop, and the splendor of all these furnishings seems slightly tarnished and artificial. The Pompeiian panels, the Argand lamps, the silver statuettes belong to a world as much sealed off from the stir of life as the tomblike chambers of Hervey's mansion in "The Return."

The creator of this world, as dominant a figure in the novel after his death as in his life, is the artist-connoisseur, Henry Allègre, who has the Goncourts' passion for collecting "brocades, pictures, bronzes, chinoiseries, japoneries" (I, 45). He is the high priest of a cult of aesthetic impressions (I, 186, 211) with its doctrine that the soul lives exclusively in sensation; and the supreme achievement of his contemptuous sacrifice of life to art is his transformation of Rita from her childhood state of a wild peasant girl of the hills to her mature position as one of the handsomest and most desirable of the objects in his house in Paris. As a model for his painting, a dummy serves him as well as a human figure (I, 22); for what matters to him is the Byzantine robe to stimulate vision and to clothe his image of the woman of all time (I, 28). After his death, however, both the dummy and the living art object that he has created remain as two awkwardly opposed consequences of his aesthetic belief and practice; for Rita, left with his fortune but deprived of his protection, ceases to be the artist's masterpiece and has to defend herself against a rapacious world. From the contrast between the mutilated dummy and the perfect harmony of Rita's appearance proceeds that note of moral irony which makes *The Arrow* as much a satire on a rigidly aesthetic philosophy as a brilliant portrayal of the milieu of the artist and his circle.

In capturing Rita as a child and placing a wall between her and mankind, Allègre performs an act similar to that of Jacobus in confining Alice to the garden in "A Smile of Fortune." But Allègre's motives are calculated to produce more ambitious results than those of the ship chandler whose imagination is limited to baiting a commercial hook for chance comers. To lift a girl out of the tide of common things at a moment when she has awakened to caprice and passion and to convert physical enchantment into a semblance of plastic art with the power to arouse and then to repel desire is Allègre's expression of the aesthete's scorn for the natural, an *épater le bourgeois* joke. In its ultimate intention, however, the deed transcends sheer mockery. To work this change, Allègre exercises a creative function in which there is something godlike in its "defiance of unexpressed things" for the "unheard-of satisfaction of an inconceivable pride" (I, 108). His whole design is characterized by "something lofty and sinister like an Olympian's caprice" (I, 108). He intends to destroy her past and to raise her by degrees to the position of a goddess of the religion of aesthetic impressions, the only faith that reigns in his studio after every other belief has been "worried into shreds" (I, 56). He attains success when he presents his idol to the world as a modern incarnation of Aphrodite with a dart, the arrow of gold in Rita's hair, a symbol of faith in the artificial and the sterile. The Olympianism of Allègre thus defies the principle of human limitation to the same extent as that of Lingard in *An Outcast*, and its failure to reckon with the problem of evil proves its insufficiency.

The perils of an aesthetic creed become evident from the moment when, after Allègre's death, Rita must descend with her treasure into the open market of the world—"a naked temperament for any wind to blow upon" (I, 84), like the stringed lute of Wilde. Through all of her commerce with the fortune hunters, blackmailers, and adventurers who cross her path in the enterprise to restore the Bourbon pretender, she retains the divinity of the charming animated statue. But a goddess or an art work, being out of time, has no past, whereas Rita's past is all too substantial. The symbol of that history, and of the fear and guilt that bind her to common humanity, is Ortega, the jealous Spaniard from her peasant childhood, who overtakes her at last as Jones overtakes Heyst in *Victory*. Her frigidity is a product of the terror inspired in her as a child by Ortega's sexual wrath (I, 112) and later by the view of mankind stripped of its clothes opened to her by Allègre (I, 96). Against this dread, felt constantly by the woman as opposed to the Mona Lisa illusion of the painter, her hysterical gesture of transfixing her hair with the golden arrow—an attempt to take cover behind the aesthetic mask—provides a simulated defense (I, 307). As if further to illuminate the contrast in Rita between the divinity and the limited human being, Conrad gives her a shadow in her sister, Therese, a peasant whose narrow and morbid mind (I, 138) and predatory instincts (I, 40) mark her as a vessel of roughest clay. Therese with the passion of greed and Ortega with that of lust are the accomplices who threaten Rita at the end as Jones and Ricardo join against Heyst.

Monsieur George, the hero who comes to defend Rita when fear compels her to drop her inscrutable smile, does not present the chivalric front of Anthony, Heyst, or Renouard but something nearer that of a guileless fool whose heart the golden arrow never pierces (I, 332). The comrade and admirer of the Ulyssean Dominic Cervoni, who scorns upper-class people but serves Rita in running guns for the Carlists, George, like Powell in *Chance*, is a member of the seaman's order and thus a believer in that common bond between men which makes him appear a "simple, innocent child of nature" (I, 70) by contrast to the corrupt society into which he is suddenly thrown. Unlike Renouard in "The Planter," George ultimately withstands the enchantment of a "mirage of desire" (I, 268) but not until he has undergone a full initiation into the life of passion and become healed of that "incurable wound" caused by his first encounter with erotic experience (I, viii, ix).

George's approach to the world ruled by a law of aesthetic impressions—his entry into the overlighted café and the bedlam of the Marseilles carnival upon his return from a long West Indian voyage—resembles the beginning of Heyst's contest with the powers of evil in the strident atmosphere of Schomberg's concert hall:

> The carnival time was drawing to an end. Everybody, high and low, was anxious to have the last fling. Companies of masks with linked arms and whooping like red Indians swept the

streets in crazy rushes while gusts of cold mistral swayed the gas lights as far as the eye could reach. There was a touch of bedlam in all this.

(I, 7)

In both scenes men accustomed to sobriety are caught by a storm of violent sensations; and Blunt and Mills, Rita's lieutenants in the Carlist plot who are attempting to enlist George's aid, complete the mischief for him by their cunning evocation of Rita as a phantom of desire in the superb Part I of *The Arrow.* The potion of exotic impressions administered to George in his ignorance of life by the two conspirators acts with the same effect that a similar drug has upon Anthony and Renouard, although here the subtler ingredients of art spice the draught. When he sees Rita for the first time on the staircase of her villa, George has been made receptive to the intense visual impression that she offers him (I, 66); and from this point he exhausts himself in the effort to penetrate beyond this illusion to the living woman with whom he feels a sense of solidarity (I, 70).

In his account of George's suffering under the spell of this wraith, Conrad not only takes every advantage of the strain of delayed consummation but also presents one of his most complete studies in the morbid psychology of passion. The process of inner destruction goes almost as far in George as in Renouard (I, 229). He falls into a "purgatory of hopeless longing" where he is tormented by exalting and cruel visions (I, 248). He reflects that his love may be a disease:

Love for Rita... if it was love, I asked myself despairingly, while I brushed my hair before a glass. It did not seem to have any sort of beginning as far as I could remember. A thing the origin of which you cannot trace cannot be seriously considered. It is an illusion. Or perhaps mine was a physical state, some sort of disease akin to melancholia which is a form of insanity?

(I, 163)

Conrad employs the pathological, however, to further his larger purpose of completing a satire on aestheticism as a doctrine at variance with normal human feeling and experience.

George breaks this spell, however, in the bizarre and melodramatic scene in the locked room in the street of the Consuls, which is both the climax of the novel and its moral denouement. Conrad wrote to Mrs. Thorne in 1919 that "the inner truth of the scene in the locked room is only hinted at," [11] thus making it clear that his intentions in this episode went beyond a winding up of the action in a spectacular way. Whatever this inner truth may have meant to Conrad, the dramatic basis of the scene viewed apart from its special atmosphere of gilt and crystal corresponds very closely to that in the cabin of the *Ferndale* in *Chance* or on Heyst's island in *Victory* in that a solitary and not wholly united man and woman are left open to the attack of an embodied force of evil. As in the earlier novels, furthermore, the preparation for this concluding act consists not so much in a knitting up of the lines of conflict between characters as in the filling out of the moral atmosphere, or the "moral topography," of the setting. Early in the story Conrad refers to the run-down and sinister appearance of the house (I, 21); and by repeated emphasis upon such interior details as the

11. Aubry, *Conrad: Life and Letters*, II, 232.

silver statuette and the black and white marble hall (I, 136), he establishes firmly both the location and the peculiar atmospheric quality of the scene. The dazzling effect of the illuminated drawing room (I, 286), the main stage for the drama, is as surprising as the revelation of its proximity to the fencing chamber with its rack of weapons. This juxtaposing of the ultrarefined and the barbaric agrees, of course, with the fantastic tone of the novel; but it is also perhaps in keeping with a book which Conrad associated with "the darkest hour of the war" (I, viii) that the rattle of steel shaken by the hand of a homicidal madman can be heard outside the door of a room designed to represent the highest flowering of art and luxury. It is unnecessary, however, to attach secondary meanings to a situation overtly symbolic with reference to the central import of the novel. At the conclusion Conrad's satire on aestheticism attains its greatest concentration as it broadens into allegory.

The movement toward the climax begins with the meeting between George and Ortega during the bedlam of the second carnival. The appearance of the Spaniard with his fixed idea of a violent assault on Rita (I, 319) and his look of a grotesque puppet (I, 267) is timed to coincide with the ebb of George's fortunes after the loss of his ship (I, 257) and with the hour of his blackest despair in his frustrated passion for Rita, very much as the ominous figure of De Barral enters the forestage in *Chance* only after Anthony has taken his vow of renunciation. Just as De Barral stands, moreover, for Anthony's double, so also Ortega seems to have a curious affinity with George. George reflects, for example, that Ortega isn't such a stranger as he had assumed he was (I, 270).

He thinks suddenly that Rita's image penetrates both himself and his companion so as to constitute a strange bond between them:

> Yes. There was between us a most horrible fellowship; the association of his crazy torture with the sublime suffering of my passion. We hadn't been a quarter of an hour together when that woman had surged up fatally between us; between this miserable wretch and myself. We were haunted by the same image. But I was sane! I was sane!
>
> (I, 274)

Rita's mockery of Ortega has turned him mad enough for passional crime; and George, though he thinks himself sane, has been brought close to the same state through her resistance to his love. While meditating upon the chance that has thrown him into association with Ortega, George concludes that "a dreadful order seemed to lurk in the darkest shadows of life" (I, 283). He appears, therefore, to catch a glimpse of a fatal train of circumstance that has brought Ortega back to confront Rita with the human passions disregarded or flouted by the doctrine taught her by Allègre. As a symbol of the evil which springs to life when the claims of normal feeling are denied, Ortega thus manifests himself to George at the moment when he has completed his initiation into the experience of passion and has seen there the face of death disclosed likewise to Anthony and Heyst in their contempt for the principle of human limits.

In terms of allegory the final scene dramatizes again the process of redemption and, as in *Chance* and *Victory*, the triumph of the normal over the abnormal. When Ortega, armed with a weapon from the fencing chamber, rattles at the doors of the locked room where Rita listens in terror, Rita's charmed cloak drops from her; and she is left a mortal woman "naked and afraid," like Hervey in "The Return," in the midst of the artificial paradise of her ornate surroundings. Observing her, George recovers from the illness of the senses in abandoning the illusion that the aesthetic image of Rita suffices for contemplation to infinity (I, 288), that it offers an escape from time and exists apart from the finite human being (I, 296). His worship of the "sublimely aesthetic impression" (I, 304) ends abruptly when Rita, at the mere whisper of Ortega's presence, springs from the couch an all too human bundle of fears with everything gone "except her strong sense of life with all its implied menaces" (I, 308). Her salvation comes through the fidelity of George in the face of danger, a safeguard which quenches her fear and rekindles a flame within her frozen body (I, 331). Drawn together by the human bond, they become once again Conrad's symbolic pair united against the evil of the world that has invaded another false Eden, the palace of art built by Allègre; and Ortega lies self-wounded at the foot of the silver statuette (I, 325).

The familiar motif of the rescue of the imperiled damsel at the conclusion of *The Arrow* is notable for the fact that the rescuer, George, having no false chivalric traits, accomplishes his task by adhering to a simple belief in love completely foreign to the highly civilized yet corrupt society in which he remains an outsider despite his temporary lapse into one of its maladies. His allegiance to the promptings of the heart emphasizes the difference between him and his rival, Captain Blunt, whose hollow scruples and nervous insomnia (I, 326–27) rob his martial pose of the dignity that should support his general pretense of knightliness. Blunt's chivalry, so highly praised by his mother, is chiefly an affair of manners; for no deeper motives than egotism and jealousy account for the discord between his impulses and the lofty idealism of his feelings and principles (I, 178). In this respect he comes close to a burlesque replica of the chivalric temperament as portrayed, for example, in the Gould of *Nostromo* whose idealism is sincere. In Blunt the fatal hero degenerates into a species of funereal statuary and chivalry into an aesthetic impression (I, 211) so that Rita dismisses him contemptuously as "the bourgeois conception of an aristocratic mourning lover" (I, 212). The ironic portrait of Blunt contributes to the satirical tone of the novel as a whole, for Conrad's depiction of upper-class characters as though they belonged in Madame Tussaud's collection of waxworks throws a harsh light upon an effete society.

The comic tone of much of *The Arrow* turns the theme of the rescuing hero, muffled though it is by Jamesian situations and aesthetic decor, into a near burlesque key; and not until *The Rescue* (1920), upon which Conrad resumed work in full earnest in 1918, does it receive a heavy tragic orchestration. No critic is likely to recommend *The Rescue* to a reader seeking for the best approach to Conrad's art. The movement of the novel is as ponderous as its length is formidable; and although the visual effects—among them the Delacroix-like panels of Lingard's parleys with the Malay chiefs in Part V—are frequently magnificent, the book as a whole is overcharged with operatic atmosphere and overweighted with an allegorical machinery which recalls its origin in the first period of Conrad's career. To *The Rescue* one must, however, turn in the end for a thorough understanding of a great source of almost all of Conrad's inspiration; for its very title, originally *The Rescuer*,[12] announces in a word the subject around which his thought constantly played. The history of the genesis and development of the story—of the difficulties of the writing; of the expansions, delays, and abandonments; of the final drive to its completion in 1919 after nearly twenty-five years of intermittent effort by Conrad and with his anticipation of death for a spur—is in itself curious and involved. If it seemed to Conrad his most refractory novel,[13] it will probably seem equally so to the reader and the critic who look for order in its complicated pattern. But while Conrad kept on with the writing of the book through practically all of his life as an author, he also seems to have drawn from its substance when he moved out along other paths of creative interest. The tremors of the explosion which at the end demolishes a world can be felt throughout the body of his work.

The conviction that *The Rescue* is the most representative, if not the most popular, of Conrad's novels grows when familiarity with the massive design makes evident what it has in common with other books written at different phases of his development. In several details the plot recalls that of *An Outcast* which Conrad conceived when he had already laid the foundation for *The Rescue*.[14] Like his namesake in *An Outcast* the Lingard of *The Rescue* aspires to pursue an

12. *Letters from Joseph Conrad: 1895–1924*, p. 46.
13. John D. Gordan, *Joseph Conrad: The Making of a Novelist*, p. 215.
14. *Ibid.*, pp. 20, 206, 226.

Edenic dream in a world of evil. His project is to restore the young Malay chieftain, Hassim, and his sister, Immada, to the rule of their native country of Wajo, from which they have been exiled by a party opposed to Hassim's succession. The force of human passion, this time within Lingard himself, intervenes, however, to nullify this aim. At the moment when Lingard's plans are maturing, a yacht belonging to a British government official named Travers is stranded on the coast near the camp where Lingard has gathered his native allies. Instead of putting the yacht afloat and sending the white people away, Lingard becomes enslaved by his admiration for Travers' wife, Edith, neglects his duty to Hassim and Immada, and ends by betraying himself and his Malay dependents in the hour when he should take absolute control of a delicate political situation. Although also a man of the common people (XII, 10–11), the hero of *The Rescue* differs, however, from the Lingard of *An Outcast* not only in being much younger but also in bringing to his idealistic scheme a chivalrous habit of mind resembling that of Gould in *Nostromo*. In his full character as a rescuer of woman in distress and as a victim of erotic feeling, the Lingard of *The Rescue* belongs to the company of the dolorous knights together with Anthony and Renouard.

Lingard's almost archetypal relationship to the rest of Conrad's fallen heroes gives to the history of his degeneration a certain universality not present in the earliest studies in failure. Together with his absurdities and his disposition to fatal blunders he contains, like Gaspar Ruiz and Nostromo, a potential of active force which wins the respect of his native followers and allies but which he spends fruitlessly in his attempt to reconcile his vow to protect Hassim and Immada with his promise to save the lives of the yacht people. The pernicious effect of imposing a sentimental code of behavior upon a capacity for objective action explains this waste, and the presentation of these opposing tendencies in Lingard adds to the general value of *The Rescue* as a guide to Conrad's thought. Lingard's fundamental attributes are sheer, almost primitive power and a need for action symbolized by his attachment to the swift brig (XII, 54) that he abandons when he takes leave forever of his own will and purpose to enter into a state of entranced immobility under Edith's spell (XII, 203). These initial capacities join with several related qualities of temperament to form what Conrad evidently regarded as the epitome of romantic individualism.

Like his forerunner in *An Outcast* Lingard has a reckless confidence in his wisdom to control human destinies and an indifference to evil suited only to omniscience. This assumption of godlike strength finds expression in his emblem of a sheaf of thunderbolts (XII, 32), a Jovian boast later ridiculed by the fall of a real thunderbolt when his powder magazine explodes and shatters his half-built world (XII, 442). Combined with this attitude of self-divinization is the chivalrous impulse which Conrad assigns to the romantic side of Lingard's nature. In a significant passage the Spaniard, D'Alcacer, who takes an observer's role as the third passenger on Travers' yacht, calls Lingard a knight, "a descendant of the immortal hidalgo errant upon the sea" (XII, 142); and Lingard's aid to the yacht people calls forth this praise. Yet his knightly behavior is no purer in its deepest motives than the idealism, grounded in vanity, that inspires his adoption of the cause of Hassim and Immada:

> He would wake up the country! That was the fundamental and unconscious emotion on which were engrafted his need of action, the primitive sense of what was due to justice, to gratitude, to friendship, the sentimental pity for the hard lot of Immada—poor child—the proud conviction that of all the men in the world, in his world, he alone had the means and the pluck "to lift up the big end" of such an adventure.
>
> (XII, 106)

His vow of fidelity to Edith Travers in her distress, by contrast to his lack of concern for the lives of Travers and D'Alcacer, is even more patently subject to erotic motivation than that of Anthony to Flora in *Chance;* and this extreme susceptibility to emotional influence makes his ruin the most abject of all suffered by Conrad's quixotic figures.

In order to project in unmistakable terms the utopian-erotic antagonism in Lingard's character, Conrad relies extensively upon his visual method of psychological description. The slow tempo of *The Rescue* results largely from the labor spent upon making the reader see, but the scenic qualities of the book are less important than the emphasis upon false vision which pertains to the major theme. The attention devoted to the eye becomes apparent not only in the opening pages where the narrative dwells upon the failure of Lingard's mate, Shaw, to observe the approach of the boat from the stranded yacht (XII, 15) but also in the more fundamental distinction between the visionary eyes of Lingard (XII, 9) and the fact-seeing ones of Carter, the young officer from the yacht (XII, 33). Conrad reserves his most telling visual reporting, however, for the two episodes wherein the awakening of Lingard's dominant impulse settles his fate.

The first of these scenes occurs when Lingard, after putting in to Hassim's village under a fierce storm, decides to save the besieged Malays. The means taken to describe not only the setting itself but also Lingard's manner of seeing the place render the event symbolic. In the flashes of lightning, the village appears "unscathed and motionless under hooked darts of flame, like some legendary country of immortals, withstanding the wrath and fire of Heaven" (XII, 80). This display of noise and fire excites Lingard much as the din in Schomberg's concert hall does Heyst, and he stands fascinated by visions of "an unknown shore":

> . . . he stood by the rail, most of the time deafened and blinded, but also fascinated, by the repeated swift visions of an unknown shore, a sight always so inspiring, as much perhaps by its vague suggestion of danger as by the hopes of success it never fails to awaken in the heart of a true adventurer. And its immutable aspect of profound and still repose, seen thus under streams of fire and in the midst of a violent uproar, made it appear inconceivably mysterious and amazing.
>
> (XII, 80)

The fact that this sight alone is enough to furnish Lingard with his initial motive for rescuing the defeated Malays testifies to his abnormally acute sensitivity. But of equal importance is the indication that this glimpse of an unknown land under the wrath of heaven takes shape for him as an imaginary vision of a lost Eden from which a human pair, Hassim and Immada, have been expelled. By one extended stroke of description Conrad exhibits, therefore, the inherent utopianism of Lingard which underlies his belief that mortal strength will suffice to restore paradise in a native village. From this peak of excitement he descends swiftly, however, to difficulties of a practical kind; for after the rescue he does not know what to do with his Adam and Eve (xii, 88).

His second experience of rapt vision comes at the meeting with Edith Travers that leaves him torn between his native and white allegiances. In his first prolonged view of her, an upper-class woman of whose type he is ignorant (xii, 304), he stands entranced "with something of the stupor of a new sensation" (xii, 141). Her blond hair appears to cast a halo round her head (xii, 139), and the effect makes him a convert to the cult of a female divinity. He takes his final vow later when, before his abandonment of the brig, he worships an illusion created by the too intense brilliance of the cabin lamp, in which light Edith looks enshrined:

> The brig's swing-lamp lighted the cabin with an extraordinary brilliance. Mrs. Travers had thrown back her hood. The radiant brightness of the little place enfolded her so close, clung to her with such force that it might have been part of her very essence. There were no shadows on her face; it was fiercely lighted, hermetically closed, of impenetrable fairness.
>
> (xii, 214)

After Lingard has looked "in unconscious ecstasy at this vision" (xii, 214), his fidelity to Hassim and Immada remains only as the memory of a once ardent ideal, since his second vision obscures the first of the unknown shore. By making bondage to desire the cause for the failure of Lingard's paradisal hopes, Conrad follows much the same pattern as he had used in *An Outcast*, where Willems' passion for Aïssa destroys the utopian dream of the older Lingard. But in *The Rescue*, where the opposing forces of idealism and eroticism meet within a single character, the conflict gains in theoretical interest; for the implication is that the two impulses spring from the same temperamental root and together account for that something "fatal and unavoidable" that Lingard feels "somewhere in the unexplored depths of his nature" and to which he attributes his confused awareness of self-betrayal (XII, 329).

As with the rest of Conrad's quixotic adventurers, Lingard's deficient understanding of the precautions necessary to the establishment of his plan complements his visionary faculty. To snatch Hassim and Immada from death and to seal the covenant of further aid upon Hassim's ring are merely the preliminaries to the harder task of keeping the pact with the native politicians, Belarab and the other chieftains, whose private schemes Lingard must favor as accessories to his own grand design. For help with this phase of his project Lingard takes for lieutenant and keeper of his powder magazine at the native settlement the ruined adventurer, Jörgenson, who becomes a main figure in the drama of superhuman ambition and human weakness. Although not villainous, Jörgenson has something in common with the earlier *döppelganger* characters in representing the dark counterpart of man's defiance of his limitations. In this phantom from the past, who resembles Lingard (XII, 112) and who sticks to him "closer than his shadow" (XII, 98), the image of disillusionment and failure inevitable on the plane of mortality moves beside the man striding in the light of self-esteem. As a result of his own disaster, which has left him dead to passion and sceptical of all enterprise, Jörgenson knows that the hazards to be run are similar to those in his old exploit; and he warns Lingard against the pact with Belarab wherein "all the devils are unchained" (XII, 103). But Lingard ignores this "inner voice" (XII, 370) which speaks of man's liability to error until after he has relinquished his independence and the command of the brig, the weapon which he needs to control his savage allies (XII, 226). His surrender to what he considers a state of supreme felicity with Edith becomes actually a descent towards Jörgenson's disenchanted realm on the dead hulk of the *Emma*, which is like a ghost of the brig that had once been Lingard's kingdom (XII, 116). Jörgenson's final blasting of the hulk, which contains everything necessary to the success of the utopian plan, seems the response of common mortality to its own frustrated effort to overreach itself.

Jörgenson destroys the material evidence of Lingard's power only, however, when he is certain that his leader's inner strength is gone and after he has taken the last step in his effort to persuade Lingard to abandon the yacht people in order to fulfil his bond with the Malays. He sends Hassim's ring to Lingard in the care of Edith Travers in the hour when, because of her complete domination of Lingard's mind and will, she controls the perilous situation which depends upon his choice between a code of chivalry and a more austere morality of honor. Her failure to deliver the ring removes the last possibility of Lingard's extricating himself from the tangle of circumstances in which he is caught; and even though he is actually beyond help, her refusal to make this gesture of fidelity proves her unwillingness to share in his tragic dilemma. As Lingard represents the romantic-chivalric temperament, so also Edith heads the feminine types of civilized decadence that can be traced back through Felicia Moorsom in "The Planter" to the girl who plays at anarchism in "The Informer." Conrad subjected her to a more minute analysis than he spent on any of his other women of this class, and perhaps for this reason she seems too often confined by a formula. Yet she is essential to the fully developed study of Lingard. Although they resemble pieces of heroic statuary, Edith and Lingard display symptoms of the same malady; and one consumes the strength of the other as they yield to the darkness of passion and death-longing (XII, 241). The quick judgment of D'Alcacer pairs them at once as victims of dreams (XII, 315).

Whereas Lingard's weakness is, however, the acceptance of dream for reality, that of Edith is her inability to see the real as anything but dream or to believe in the existence of anyone or anything outside herself. This extreme subjectivism counts as a main flaw in so marked a European type as Edith who seems made for action (XII, 139). Because she suffers, like Heyst, from disenchantment, Lingard spends his passion vainly in the effort to draw her into his own exotic world. A prey to ennui (XII, 457) and to spiritual emptiness under the material glory seen by Lingard, she cannot conceive of the world except in its phenomenal aspect, either as an aesthetic spectacle or as a painted cloth hiding reality. For this reason the realm of intense experience with its issues of life and death and its councils of war to which Lingard admits her at his Settlement takes on for her no other significance than that of a stage curtain (XII, 260). She regards the people as sketches in color and the events deciding the fate of a kingdom as a barbarous pageant, the reality of which she cannot feel:

> She saw, she imagined, she even admitted now the reality of those things no longer a mere pageant marshalled for her vision with barbarous splendor and savage emphasis. She questioned it no longer—but she did not feel it in her soul any more than one feels the depth of the sea under its peaceful glitter or the turmoil of its grey fury.
>
> (XII, 367)

In the scenes at the Settlement which lead to the climax of the book, Conrad transfers the point of view chiefly to Edith not only to enhance the brilliant tones of the description, as these strike her inexperienced eye, but also to exhibit her psychological traits by the most concrete method. His management of visual devices in this section of the novel is expert, and it adds substance to one of his most acute studies in mental detachment.

Like the ultracivilized characters in the stories of the *Nostromo* phase, Edith displays an inclination to dally with violence as a substitute for personal experience with the deeper emotions of humanity. Since her marriage to Travers has brought her no opportunity for sincerity or true feeling (XII, 152), she places undue value upon the picturesque externals of Lingard's adventure in order to derive from it the most complete enjoyment of new and exciting sensations (XII, 162). With something like the longing for the primitive found in people in the work of D. H. Lawrence, for "the naked truth of life and passion buried under the growth of centuries" (XII, 153), she envies the Malay girl, Immada, and at the Settlement costumes herself in the latter's clothes of a princess (XII, 274). But in all of her attempts to feel heroic, to imagine herself a woman in a ballad (XII, 216), she never loses the conviction that she is acting in a play. She resembles Felicia Moorsom in "The Planter of Malata" in that she cannot respond to life and passion even when Lingard makes it possible for her to experience both in their most obvious form:

> "I mean the morning when I walked out of Belarab's stockade on your arm, Captain Lingard, at the head of the procession. It seemed to me that I was walking on a splendid stage in a scene from an opera, in a gorgeous show fit to make an audience hold its breath. You can't possibly guess how unreal all this seemed, and how artificial I felt myself. An opera, you know. . . ."
>
> (XII, 300)

Since Edith's numbness in feeling is the opposite extreme from Lingard's overexcitability in this respect, the two characters become symbolic of that division in modern temperament which for so long engaged Conrad's attention. The lack of understanding between Edith, as a woman of the upper class, and Lingard, as a man of the common people, adds a social element to Conrad's theme of the disunited human pair.

This theme emerges, however, through denser allegorical complications than those, for example, in *Victory* or "The Planter"—complications due mainly to Conrad's introduction of so many secondary characters to dramatize to the full the governing idea of the wreck of man's paradisal hopes upon the necessities of a fallen world. The parallel relationship between the two couples of Edith and Lingard and Hassim and Immada offers one illustration of this point; for the chance of the Malays regaining their kingdom depends upon the continuance of Lingard's fidelity to the innocent Immada, as opposed to the tempted Eve in Edith, or upon the foredoomed hope of Lingard and Edith joining in united action. After the intrusion of the yacht people into Lingard's history Hassim and Immada follow in the path of the white couple as though symbolic of an ideal of the human pair established in actuality, of what Edith and Lingard might accomplish by accepting the challenge of the bond of the ring to a deed to be fulfilled in a world of error. It is understandable, therefore, that the removal of Lingard and Edith from the brig and their descent into the night of passion draw Hassim and Immada into the same poisonous atmosphere (XII, 240). In the fact, recognized by D'Alcacer, that Edith and Lingard seem made for each other (XII, 310), like the equally extraordinary Felicia and Renouard in "The Planter," lies the foundation, at least, for a league to restore the only Eden possible to man and woman in their fallen state, could they understand that love which enables Lena in *Victory* to combat evil. But the self-abasement of Lingard before the image of Edith and her own rejection of the life impulse in him (XII, 395) leave them defenseless before the will to negation in Jörgenson which obliterates Lingard's work and returns his world to the satanic powers of Belarab and his allies.

As a mere adventurer, despite his titles of "King Tom" and "Rajah Laut," Lingard proves, therefore, as untrustworthy a redeemer as "Lord" Jim at Patusan; and the references to his "standing upon the sea" (XII, 153) or coming to Edith "like a thief in the night" (XII, 398) invite the same ironical interpretation as the Biblical allusions in *An Outcast* or *Typhoon.* A measure for his defiance of human limitation is the young seaman, Carter, who occupies a small, clearly lighted space in the broad canvas of the novel. Carter's respect for Lingard's strength does not modify his judgment that the older man is too audacious (XII, 50), that his adventure is unsound (XII, 187), and that his refusal to give up a muddled enterprise is bad (XII, 183). Carter alone among the characters derives any benefit from the turmoil around Lingard in that he receives an initiation into responsibility (XII, 426); and when, after Lingard's collapse, he succeeds to the command of the brig, he confirms—like Powell in *Chance* —the triumph of the normal over the abnormal. But the triumph brings nothing more than the quiet of exhaustion over a world robbed of color (XII, 425) and mute under the rising shadow of the night.

When, in the final scene, Edith and Lingard meet for the last time on an arid sandbank (XII, 460) in the midst of a void of silence (XII, 463), they speak like phantoms in a wasteland. So tainted is the universe with utter debility and defeat that *The Rescue* can, perhaps, be regarded as more prophetic for a society on the aftermath of the First World War than its plot and background immediately suggest. The fall of Lingard signifies something more momentous than the betrayal of a Devon fisherman through vanity and passion; and of this profounder meaning Edith obtains a glimpse in her dream of Lingard as a Crusader disappearing among barbarians:

> She woke up, with her face wet with tears, out of a vivid dream of Lingard in chain-mail armour and vaguely recalling a Crusader, but bare-headed and walking away from her in the depths of an impossible landscape. She hurried on to catch up with him but a throng of barbarians with enormous turbans came between them at the last moment and she lost sight of him forever in the flurry of a ghastly sand-storm. What frightened her most was that she had not been able to see his face. It was then that she began to cry over her hard fate.
>
> (xii, 458)

In the retreat of this knightly figure, pursued vainly by Edith, Conrad seems to record the passing of a chivalric tradition in the funeral march conclusion of *The Rescue*. Although a confusion of aims dissipates his power, Lingard might have achieved the victory of life over death in the restoration of man and woman to their rightful kingdom. In *The Rover*, with a hero who affirms a different code of values than the erotic-chivalric, Conrad frees the life principle for the accomplishment of this task.

As though he had finished with his long treatment of degeneration in the Lingard type of character, Conrad changed his scene in *The Rover* (1923) to France during the Revolutionary and Napoleonic periods. The novel marks, therefore, the beginning of his occupation with the historical subject that interested him until his death. But just as the Napoleonic background for his earlier story, "The Duel," provides an appropriate atmosphere for the moral and psychological issue, so also the historical milieu in *The Rover*, although it affects the motives and behavior of the characters, compels attention less than the "moral topography" and the symbolic pattern which show the close thematic relationship between this novel and the rest of the work of the last phase. Because of its graceful style and simple plot *The Rover* presents at first, and by contrast to the tangled allegory of *The Rescue*, a deceptively idyllic appearance which is no more than the even light shed by Conrad's mature reflection over a tale of tragic circumstance and bitter sacrifice.

If *The Rescue* stands as the fullest expression of Conrad's distrust of a false chivalric ideal, *The Rover* may be seen as one of his strongest affirmations—almost a parable, in fact—of the superiority of life over death, of the normal over the abnormal. Where *The Rescue* ends, in a wasteland, the main action of *The Rover* begins—in the arid, salt-impregnated desert of the Giens Peninsula (xxiv, 14–15) and the sea-girt Escampobar Farm with its terrified women and its bloodthirsty master. The hero who descends into this abandoned landscape to accomplish later the redemption of another distressed human pair has no trace of the quixotic in his manner and no ambition except for a quiet place of rest out of men's sight (xxiv, 12). An old man, wounded (xxiv, 6) and mounted upon a hired mule (xxiv, 14), the former seaman Peyrol, might be the strength of Lingard wholly divested of its romantic armor and its crest of thunderbolts.

In returning to the place of his birth after a lifetime of adventurous wandering in Eastern waters, Peyrol decides to make his home at the Escampobar Farm because he is attracted to the girl, Arlette, who lives there with her Aunt Catherine in dependence upon the owner of the place, Scevola, a notorious sans-culotte who has brought the spirit of the Terror to the region. Scevola has gained control of the farm through the death of its former owners, Arlette's mother and father, royalists killed in the Toulon Massacre of several years before. Not actually a revolutionary but a pathological case and a creature of mob psychology,[15] Scevola is a man whom no amount of killing can satisfy (xxiv, 27); and his sadism inflames his desire for Arlette even in the half-insane condition in which he has brought her back from witnessing her parents' death at Toulon. Catherine has succeeded in protecting Arlette; but at the time of Peyrol's arrival the state of affairs at the farm has become critical both because of Scevola's growing impatience and Arlette's newly awakened love for the naval lieutenant, Réal, who comes to Escampobar in order to spy upon the movements of the British fleet against which he has been ordered to carry out a secret mission. By force of character Peyrol maintains order, soothing Arlette's unrest and standing between the frightened women and the crazed Scevola whom Peyrol holds in contempt. In order to make possible Arlette's complete return to sanity through union with Réal, Peyrol in the end assumes the lieutenant's duty of carrying false dispatches which will fall into the hands of Nelson and so deceive the British admiral with regard to the operations of the French fleet. Having fitted out the abandoned tartane once used to carry Arlette's parents to their death in Toulon and the girl herself back to the farm, Peyrol locks Scevola in the cabin, accomplishes his task, and dies in the Mediterranean under enemy fire.

Peyrol's sacrifice of his life removes Scevola, who has cast the blight of the Fall over Escampobar, and frees the

15. Aubry, *Conrad: Life and Letters*, II, 326–27.

land for inheritance by Réal and Arlette. Yet despite its tranquil conclusion and the brave death of Peyrol after the exciting chase of the tartane by the British corvette, the story is not a quiet historical romance. As in Conrad's earlier works in this phase there is emphasis in *The Rover* upon suffering and fatality. Like the heroines that precede her, Arlette has been mentally injured at Toulon by the shock of encountering "terrors comparable to those of the Judgment Day" (XXIV, 145) and left in a state of hysterical "possession," which Conrad describes with his usual careful attention to pathological detail. Little more than a child and "smitten on the very verge of womanhood" by a fear always threatening to take form as a "mutilated vision of the dead" (XXIV, 49), she remains in a condition almost identical with that of Flora de Barral after the latter's exposure to the passion of the governess. With Flora, moreover, Arlette shares not only the misfortune of a psychic wound but also the dubious gift of the persecuted maiden: the enhancement of physical charm by the malady of fear (XXIV, 150). If the beautiful and the morbid are not so plainly associated in *The Rover* as in *Chance*, their meeting in Arlette accounts in great part for her appeal to Scevola's desire as well as for the repugnance felt at the outset by her lover, Réal, towards what he regards as a body without mind (XXIV, 214). Scevola himself, though too cowardly to offer any real danger to a man like Peyrol, carries with him the shadow of perverse and homicidal impulse; and as an embodiment of the evils of fear, lust, and violence, he completes the line of grotesque villains extending from Heemskirk through Ortega.

Even though clear-sighted and sound in nerve, Peyrol too

is not spared his draught of bitterness; and at the end he chooses death in order to avoid a temptation to become the moral equal of Scevola. In returning to France, Peyrol steps at once into a net of tragic circumstance spread for him at Escampobar. He takes quarters at the farm in the illusion that he may attain peace and a home for his "instinct of rest" (XXIV, 31). But at his first meeting with Arlette, he feels for the girl "a kind of intimate emotion which he had not known before to exist by itself in a man" (XXIV, 88). This paternal affection, in a character hitherto ignorant of sentiment (XXIV, 34), enters into Peyrol's feeling of attachment to the farm as well as into the jealousy inspired in him by the appearance of Réal. Because of Arlette's confidence in him Peyrol has been able to work the first miracle leading to her recovery of sanity (XXIV, 169), but the process completes itself by the awakening of her passion for her lover which flames out into a brilliance of life that staggers Peyrol when it strikes his eyes (XXIV, 174). The scene in which he stands dazzled by the transformation in Arlette from a child mute with terror to a woman enhaloed with vitality resembles that in *The Rescue* where Lingard forgets himself under the spell cast by Edith Travers in the cabin of the brig. Intense physical enchantment robs Peyrol of strength, and the still active feelings of vigorous age supply fuel to his emotion:

> She dazzled him. Vitality streamed out of her eyes, her lips, her whole person, enveloped her like a halo and . . . yes, truly, the faintest possible flush had appeared on her cheeks, played on them faintly rosy like the light of a distant flame on the snow. She raised her arms up in the air and let her hands fall from on high on Peyrol's shoulders, captured his desperately

dodging eyes with her black and compelling glance, put out all her instinctive seduction—while he felt a growing fierceness in the grip of her fingers.

(XXIV, 175)

This new stimulus to the sentiment existing in him so long unobserved sharpens the internal conflict which distracts him in the crisis of choice between sending Réal to death in the tartane and assuming the lieutenant's odious duty himself (XXIV, 237). The fact that he decides quickly for the second alternative does not obscure the point that the decision itself, like that faced by Lingard, lies between the claims of a human pair and those of personal desire. Arlette's dream of Réal sinking under the blows of a murderous crowd while Peyrol ignores her cries for help indicates how strongly the temptation to betrayal sways Peyrol momentarily (XXIV, 246). In that moment he verges on spiritual complicity with Scevola, as George in *The Arrow* walks for a time with the homicidal Ortega; and even after he has stilled this prompting to serve death rather than life, he carries on his last journey the memory of a veil of peace "torn down by the touch of a sentiment unexpected like an intruder and cruel like an enemy" (XXIV, 268).

Although he refuses to be humiliated like Conrad's knightly rescuers and would-be saviors, Peyrol smarts, nevertheless, under the lash of genuine passion, the more cruel for its violation of age; and he gains freedom only by acceptance of his fate. The novel would not conform as it does to the spirit of Conrad's work were not Peyrol's restitution of the normal to some degree a stoical acquiescence in the cruelty of life and a casting off of the illusion of tranquillity. His adherence to life over death, to action as opposed to passivity—two great alternatives in Conrad's habit of thought—brings for reward only an existence honorably closed and clarity of vision to life's perpetual unrest. To assume that Peyrol's motive for sacrifice is merely that of love for Arlette or of patriotism would be to narrow the issue to sentimental grounds not consistent with the temper of the man himself. His choice has the quality of defiance—to his own momentary weakness, to the fate which has tricked him into an emotional snare, perhaps even to all of life's petty deceptions in the light of which a resolute death may seem superior to the cause whose furtherance that death obtains. In this respect the end of Peyrol's career is, curiously enough, not unlike that of Almayer; for the same sort of triangular relationship involving a paternal figure and two young lovers exists in Conrad's last complete novel as in his first. Except that Peyrol wills his own death in the strong consciousness of what life demands whereas Almayer is trampled down by the procreative force that he despises, both men break decisively with all that concerns the blind functioning of nature; and this renunciation,[16] simply as an attitude of mind, appears to surpass in dignity the love of the young man and woman left to continue the cycle of human experience. Although the clear sunlight of heroic action bathes the end of *The Rover* rather than the gloom of tropical decay hanging over the conclusion to *Almayer's Folly*,

16. Conrad speaks favorably on renunciation in his essay, "Henry James."—III: *Notes on Life and Letters*, 16, 18.

it is a light passing from the sadness of the land to the impersonal plain of the sea, as though accompanying the tartane and her intrepid commander beyond the strife of men and the world of chance.

The last of Conrad's rescuers is, therefore, also the first who does not himself need a savior; and the Biblical allusions throughout the book seem to apply to him without irony. Yet, as his whole behavior at Escampobar makes clear, Peyrol has no conception of himself as finer or more powerful than ordinary men. Strength enables him to remove the evil spell upon the land, but this attribute serves him only because it is supported by other qualities derived from an early initiation into the harshest experience. Having known the savagery of nature and of human beings (XXIV, 24), having been tried by passion and betrayal, he has in his soul a drop of scorn that clarifies his vision of the limited resources of men as opposed to the enduring malevolence of the world:

> What he had gone through, from a spell of crazy love for a yellow girl to the experience of treachery from a bosom friend and shipmate (and both those things Peyrol confessed to himself he could never hope to understand), with all the graduations of varied experience of men and passions between, had put a drop of universal scorn, a wonderful sedative, into the strange mixture which might have been called the soul of the returned Peyrol.
>
> (XXIV, 25)

This scepticism, a good preventive against the kind of romantic disillusionment suffered by Lingard, awakens Peyrol's contempt for the ideals of the French Revolution which he defines curtly as "certain Immortal Principles causing the death of many people" (xxiv, 25).[17] This phrase re-echoes much that Conrad himself says in condemning revolution as a stimulant to human cravings for blood and death; and it seems possible that in *The Rover* he turned back to the Revolutionary period not only for new literary material but also to reach the source of a doctrine of human supremacy, with its consequences in the misery of the Escampobar Farm, to which he could oppose his own myth of fall and redemption.

As the image of a victorious man from the sea Peyrol appears, then, to mirror Conrad's personal assertion of the modern desire for a hero who is both paternal and invincible in his contest with the powers of darkness. As an almost archetypal figure with his roots in that soil of common humanity which Conrad thought an essential basis for a society becoming morbidly attracted to perversity and violence, Peyrol conserves and employs the strength wasted in such characters as Gaspar Ruiz, Nostromo, and Lingard. He becomes, therefore, an interesting substitute for the declining chivalric type. Although the myth of the redemption of a wasted land appears plainly enough in *The Rover*, the rescuer is Ulyssean rather than knightly—as such features of the story as Peyrol's return home after long wandering, the Telemachus-like situation of Réal, and the final launching forth of the old hero to renewed toil upon the sea obviously suggest. When he drew Peyrol, a thorough Latin with Roman features (xxiv, 5) and a native of that Mediterranean coast which is an appropriate setting for a novel built so

17. Conrad said of the French Revolution: "The glorified French Revolution itself, except for its destructive force, was in essentials a mediocre phenomenon."—III: *Notes on Life and Letters*, 86.

closely on the theme of renewed life, Conrad seems to have recalled his parting glimpse in *The Mirror of the Sea* of that companion of his youth, Dominic Cervoni, turning away in the very guise of Ulysses.

In *The Rover* and at a point in his life when he was preparing to clear decks before going below for the last time, Conrad defined an ideal of conduct for man in a fallen world; and on this ground the novel deserves study in relation to the whole of his work. To create the curious figure of Peyrol, who is both piratical and Christlike, Conrad drew upon some source of inspiration which had little to do with time; for Peyrol does not really belong to the world of Dominic Cervoni or of Allistoun in *The Nigger*, though he has some of the virtues of these men, any more than he belongs to the world of Napoleonic France to which he returns as a stranger. He has been a member, however, of a "strange fraternity," the Brothers of the Coast (xxiv, 8)—a kind of primitive clan with nothing of the mystical or the chivalric in its organization. It is possible, therefore, that he reflects a measure of scepticism on Conrad's part with regard to the whole idea of chivalry as well as a premonition of the ultimate decline of this great traditional legend of the Western world, a view which anticipates that of T. S. Eliot in *The Waste Land*. Apprehension of this kind may account for the note of melancholy that accompanies Conrad's ironical treatment of his defeated knights, who are so often, like the Don of Cervantes, extraordinary characters. The fact that these men are generally of Nordic stock may likewise point to some association in Conrad's mind between chivalric idealism and a Nordic tendency to prefer the abstract to the concrete, for he speaks in *Nostromo* of "the misty idealism of the Northerners" by contrast to the "clear-minded Southern races" (IX, 333). It is notable, in any case, that the heroism of sentimentalists and dreamers like Jasper Allen, Anthony, Heyst, and Lingard is tinged with absurdity, whereas that of men of Mediterranean origin like Dominic Cervoni and Peyrol wins praise.

The fallen knights in Conrad's last stories are not, however, any more truly chivalrous than the hermits in his first are ascetic. Their impulse to act, to rescue the unfortunate, runs out into channels of perversity or sensuality which negate the purposes of life; and in the measure that they deviate from the norm of conduct, they meet the proof of their exile from paradise in the forms of evil that attack them. In his final phase, therefore, Conrad went to the heart of his earlier theme of limitation by turning to the subject of sex; and in his clearest allegories, in *Chance* and *Victory*, he placed the human pair at the center of his paradisal setting. Against the background of a fallen Eden he distinguished between attitudes in love which deny and those which affirm the task of man and woman to defend their small world; and the cultivation of the erotic for its own sake, the love-death impulse, he portrayed with his sharpest irony. In these later books, and at particular length in *The Rescue*, he displays remarkable insight into evidences of decay in the society of his age; and in his own fashion he recognizes as acutely as G. B. Shaw the problem of sexual morality in a time of shifting values.

The work of Conrad's last years gives full evidence of his ability as a psychologist in literature and as a witness to the dangers of confused understanding in matters of life and death. In this phase, moreover, he reveals more clearly than in his earlier writing the ideal of action in accordance with the needs of ordinary mankind; for although he dwells upon the absurdities and evils that result from attempts to follow impulses other than those which are native to man in his precarious state as a fallen being, he establishes a basis of reference to the norm of conduct in characters like Powell, Lena, George, Carter, and Peyrol. At times the intellectual interest of his later books is stronger than their hold upon the reader's imagination, largely, perhaps, because he came to rely more upon conscious contrivance than in his earlier stories. The minutely worked out and sometimes overly involved allegorical situations seem to testify to this point. But in the final stage of his career he had a firm grasp upon his major themes and the sure control of his medium necessary to bring them to a consummation. His steady vision in these years of the importance of traditional human values in a century of growing unrest and confusion gave added force to his great endowment in artistic power.

Chapter 5

CONCLUSION

The Shadow Line

DURING the last three months of 1916[1] and in a mood deeply influenced by his thought of "the supreme trial of a whole generation" (XVII, viii), Conrad wrote *The Shadow Line*, one of the greatest of his works and a departure from the rest of his later books both in its omission of the theme of erotic misfortune and in its avoidance of extreme technical ingenuity. The story, as he informs the reader, is complex (XVII, vii)—not, like *Chance*, in structure but in conception, after the manner of such other tales devoted wholly to the experience of seamen as *The Nigger* and "The Secret Sharer." The subtitle, *A Confession*, distinguishes the story further from the mass of Conrad's novels and relates in an intimate way to his personal life:

From my statement that I thought of this story for a long time under the title of "First Command" the reader may guess that it is concerned with my personal experience. And as a matter of

1. Conrad, XVII: *The Shadow Line*, ix.

fact it *is* personal experience seen in perspective and colored by that affection one can't help feeling for such events of one's life as one has no reason to be ashamed of.

(XVII, ix)

So pronounced, in fact, is its motif of guilt and absolution that the writing may have served a genuinely confessional purpose in relieving Conrad's spirit of some part of the burden of that dark year of war.

Despite manifold implications the story finds root in the theme of the continuity of human life and of tradition, an idea asserted here more directly than elsewhere in Conrad's work perhaps because of his reflection on the breach in human solidarity caused by the war. His conviction of "the intimate delicacies of our relation to the dead and to the living, in their countless multitudes" (XVII, vii–viii) not only speaks out in the Author's Note but also wells up from time to time in the narrative itself. This principle likewise governs the logic of the central episode in the story, the narrator's inner crisis which begins at a moment of transition from youth to maturity and severs temporarily the bond uniting him to his profession. In order that he may learn the meaning and value of continuity, he must undergo an experience of isolated spiritual conflict before acquiring the power of command in its related aspects of control of the self and of the assumption of responsibility for the defense of a tradition. The drifting of his becalmed ship followed by its rapid flight on a charted course at the end of his ordeal are evocative supporting images for the topic of continuity broken and restored.

In accordance with a familiar practice by Conrad the action begins with an irrational or capricious move: the young narrator's sudden resignation from his comfortable mate's berth on an Eastern steamer (XVII, 4). His only known motive for this act is his Hamlet-like feeling that the world is stale and unprofitable (XVII, 28), his seafaring existence "a dreary, prosaic waste of days" (XVII, 7). So pervasive, however, is this spirit of discontent that it separates him from the fellowship of seamen as well as from the "enchanted garden" of youth (XVII, 3), the Eden from which he falls into a world of evil. His retreat to the tomblike Officers' Home and to the company of men who have become torpid resembles Jim's withdrawal to shore life before he signs on with the *Patna;* for, like Jim, the narrator knows nothing as yet of the possible consequences of the step he has taken. His story involves, therefore, a gradual process of discovery not only that life includes a greater range of marvels and terrors than he has imagined but also that there are secret motives of conduct with which he has never reckoned.

What he cannot perceive—that other side of his nature which is dominated by the irrational—exposes itself to Captain Giles, the elderly sailor who can see the inside of most things (XVII, 38) and who befriends the outcast. Giles, whose paternal manner arouses the narrator's resentment, possesses certain Ulyssean traits—his expertness in intricate navigation (XVII, 12), his reputation for wonderful adventures and a mysterious tragedy in his life (XVII, 14)—which are in keeping with his role of initiating figure about to launch the narrator on a journey into a realm of darkness. Giles takes a solemn view of the young mate much as Marlow does of Jim, for there is a similarity between Jim's inability to regard himself as one with the other *Patna* officers and the mate's unreadiness to recognize himself as a new member of the circle of castaways at the Home. Not, in fact, until he awakens to the underhand game intended to cheat him of the command awaiting him, his first encounter with human malice (XVII, 37), does the narrator catch a glimpse of the truth that he is involved in evil and has contributed by his own indifference to the harm done him. Conrad makes skillful use of his ironical method in this section of *The Shadow Line*, for the reader is able to contrast the narrator's illusion that Giles is insane (XVII, 21) with the latter's distrust of the sanity of the mate. The distressing moment of self-revelation arrives for the narrator on the eve of his passage into the death-haunted atmosphere of the Gulf of Siam.

The first turning point in the story is the scene where the narrator, promoted as if by a miracle from the status of mate to that of captain, sits facing himself in the cabin mirror of the sailing ship that he has been assigned to take through the Gulf into the open sea. All that happened to him before being thrust into this position of responsibility has formed a sequence of events remarkable enough to enlarge his knowledge but also so abrupt that its import comes home only in this interlude of introspection. The cabin is the appropriate setting for this occasion; for when he seats himself in the captain's chair and assumes a commander's powers and duties, he remains no longer the unreflective young mate but becomes a different man by virtue of his return to the traditions of the sea. He has reached a stage where he can survey his immediate past from the same point occupied previously by Giles. Exalted by his good luck, he awakens for the first time to the meaning of the bond between the living and the dead within a tradition:

> A succession of men had sat in that chair. I became aware of that thought suddenly, vividly, as though each had left a little of himself between the four walls of these ornate bulkheads; as if a sort of composite soul, the soul of command, had whispered suddenly to mine of long days at sea and of anxious moments.
>
> (XVII, 52–53)

He regards himself also as the latest member of a dynasty with a traditional point of view on life:

> And I stared back at myself with the perfect detachment of distance, rather with curiosity than with any other feeling, except of some sympathy for this latest representative of what for all intents and purposes was a dynasty; continuous not in blood, indeed, but in its experience, in its training, in its conception of duty, and in the blessed simplicity of its traditional point of view on life.
>
> (XVII, 53)

Almost simultaneously, however, another and very different face, intently watching, looms up beside the commander's image in the mirror—that of the mate, Burns, whose silent entry and fixed gaze annoy the Captain (XVII, 54). The mate appears as unexpectedly as an apparition; and his sudden intrusion upon the Captain's privacy recalls the entrance, in somewhat similar circumstances, of Leggatt in "The Secret Sharer" or of Haldin in *Under Western Eyes.* Conrad's doubling machinery seems to operate again here with the introduction of Burns as a concrete semblance of that other self that the Captain could not see on shore, the past that haunts him in his solitude. In this man of ghastly and pugnacious physiognomy (xvii, 53), who reminds the Captain of the youth that he has left behind and makes him self-conscious (xvii, 55), the Captain confronts at last the face seen by Giles behind the confident mask of the young mate at the Home. And Burns is a sick man; for although, like the Captain, a good seaman (xvii, 63), he suffers from a mental ailment which must be cured before he can take his place at the commander's right hand.

The Captain's second surprise comes with the revelation by Burns of the character of the late master of the ship, who before his death had frightened the mate into a condition near to insanity. As described at length by Burns, this "old captain" appears an embodiment of illness, irrationality, and the life-hatred expressed in his desire to lose the ship with all hands. He has ended his life by a betrayal of the tradition that the young commander now believes in so ardently:

> And like a member of a dynasty, feeling a semi-mystical bond with the dead, I was profoundly shocked by my immediate predecessor.
>
> That man had been in all essentials but his age just such another man as myself. Yet the end of his life was a complete act of treason, the betrayal of a tradition which seemed to me as imperative as any guide on earth could be. It appeared that even at sea a man could become the victim of evil spirits. I felt on my face the breath of unknown powers that shape our destinies.
>
> (xvii, 62)

Since the old captain has also been a "predecessor" in the line of seamen, as much so as Giles except for the difference between a master of the art of navigation and a man who has finished his career as a Flying Dutchman (XVII, 94), the depressing tale told by Burns may well fill the narrator's mind with doubt of the holding power of a tradition, the problem that troubled Marlow in *Lord Jim.*

The story from Burns gives the Captain sufficient cause to interpret his former resentment of Giles as a secret allegiance to a view of life corresponding to that of the old captain, a secret compact with unreason, despair, and death which constitutes a betrayal of tradition. By this means, after his acquaintance with the sick and frightened other self in Burns, the Captain obtains a still deeper understanding of the true grounds for the revolt that he had associated vaguely with feelings of discontent and life-emptiness. By tracing the link between Burns and the dead man, fear inspired by an irrational force, the Captain has before him a mental diagram of his own earlier conduct.

The delusion that has mastered Burns and that his fever aggravates is a "fixed idea" (XVII, 82) that death has not ended the evil of the old captain but that the latter continues from his burial place in the Gulf to cast over the ship a spell which will destroy both the new captain and the crew (XVII, 74). Since Conrad notes that this is no more than a superstitious fancy (XVII, viii), it may be regarded as a false opinion of life and of tradition—a view that the dead exercise a malevolent influence upon the living or that death is superior to life. Although the Captain, with his restored faith, attempts to combat this error by insisting to Burns that the dead feel no animosity against the living (XVII, 82), the notion troubles him and menaces his common sense because it defines the confusion of values that had prompted him to abandon the sea. The subservience of Burns to the old captain and his doubt of the new, therefore, mirrors the attitude of the narrator in his transition from youth to maturity. His struggle to free himself from the errors of his past contributes to his anguish in the Gulf and runs parallel to the slow recovery of Burns in his progress towards the world of "living men" (XVII, 84).

Except for the fact that the Captain is not alone in his ordeal, his experience in the calm and the smothering darkness of the Gulf with the ship helplessly "poised on the edge of some violent issue, lurking in the dark" (XVII, 115) resembles that of Jim immediately after the accident to the *Patna.* In both episodes men whose spiritual resistance has been weakened endure an extreme test in which strength of soul is the only resource, since external events confound the senses and bend the reason to an acceptance of the mad logic of circumstance. An aspect of nature outside predictable control, perilous, and hitherto unknown to them presents itself to both men and by complementing in its own disorder the irrational within the individual adds to their confusion and reflects their despair. In his last conversation with Giles, who warns him that the Gulf is "a funny piece of water" (XVII, 44), the Captain shows no concern about entering this region since it belongs to a general territory that has become familiar to him. But his direct exposure to the fluctuating weather of the Gulf brings with it the same shock of the unknown given him by his glimpse into the deeps of his own nature, and what he meets in the outer world takes form as a symbol of his own inner darkness and division. Before his vigil ends, he suffers a "moral dissolution" which threatens to rob him of his sanity and to compel his surrender to the mate's delusion that he is the creature of the old captain. In the malicious and unaccountable play of circumstances he begins to observe a purposeful malevolence (XVII, 87), a "horrid logic" (XVII, 93), like that which seemed operative in the *Patna* disaster; and his discovery that the old captain has tampered with the quinine needed by the sick members of the crew precipitates a crisis wherein he feels the weight of the old captain's dead hand (XVII, 89). The impatient words of his diaries (XVII, 97) and the upsurge of joy that he feels when the dead calm ends with the breaking of the first ridge of foam along the keel of the ship express the Captain's loathing of this stagnation and his desire to return to the normal tempo of existence (XVII, 121). When at last he goes ashore again, he marvels, like a convalescent, at the strong vitality of everyone he meets (XVII, 130).

Effective in conveying the sense of arrested life are the images of chaos and creation which can be related to the general background of cosmic metaphor in Conrad's work. The Captain's longing to pass the belt of calm aims not only at the resumption of movement but also at a renewal of the feeling of creative effort which the stillness destroys. On the first evening of the outward voyage the Captain sees around him a void in which his command seems to fly like a planet:

> After sunset I came out on deck again to meet only a still void. The thin, featureless crust of the coast could not be distinguished. The darkness had risen around the ship like a mysterious emanation from the dumb and lonely waters. I leaned on the rail and turned my ear to the shadows of the

night. Not a sound. My command might have been a planet flying vertiginously on its appointed path in a space of infinite silence.

(XVII, 73–74)

Although this is the same kind of planetary metaphor as that applied to the ship in *The Nigger*, its use in *The Shadow Line* enhances the specific impression that the becalmed vessel is a world floating in the midst of primeval chaos, especially at the crisis where the rain and darkness blot out every light (XVII, 114). As the tension gathers in the perfect immobility of the elements, the Captain thinks of the end of all things:

When the time came the blackness would overwhelm silently the bit of starlight falling upon the ship, and the end of all things would come without a sigh, stir, or murmur of any kind, and all our hearts would cease to beat like run-down clocks.

It was impossible to shake off that sense of finality. The quietness that came over me was like a foretaste of annihilation. It gave me a sort of comfort, as though my soul had become suddenly reconciled to an eternity of blind stillness.

(XVII, 108)

The sound of the rain sweeping into the silence of this "darkness before creation" (XVII, 113) in which the beating of terrified hearts has become almost audible announces a baptismal ceremony—the exorcism of fear and superstition in Burns (XVII, 124) and a removal of the afflictions that have tempered the Captain's soul for the responsibility of command (XVII, 129). For this deliverance the Captain owes everything to the help of Ransome, the consummate seaman with the failing heart, who is so plainly the adversary of

Burns in this allegory of psychological and spiritual conflict. Although Ransome's fidelity to duty and his intelligent and serene temperament sustain the Captain (XVII, 112), his strength of soul, which the delusion of Burns cannot impair, offers the young commander an example of the one resource that proves dependable at a time when the mind turns helpless (XVII, 112). Ransome thus exhibits in a simplified but dramatic form a quality which Conrad had singled out as a basis for faith in stories as early as "An Outpost of Progress" and "Heart of Darkness." The Captain's experience has prepared him to revalue life on Ransome's humble terms, those of a man who finds life a boon and who must, therefore, guard constantly against the danger of real death that he carries in his heart (XVII, 129). In this light Ransome provides a clearly drawn image of man's estate as Conrad habitually regards it—in its simple grandeur of fidelity to a tradition of duty and in its misery of the fragile human heart. Man is mortal and should act with conscious knowledge of this mortality. That is both the idea that Ransome leaves his captain to contemplate and the conviction that determines Conrad's attitude to the spectacle of life.

Ransome's humility exemplifies once again that belief in human limitation which emerges throughout Conrad's writing as a corollary to his central allegorical themes of Fall and lost Eden. Like most of his stories, *The Shadow Line* is a tale of the loss of innocence and illusion, of the narrator's descent from an almost paradisal state ordered as though by a "benevolent Enchanter" (XVII, 5) into a world of chance and error, failure, sickness, and death. A man's first open encounter with evil, an experience shaped in the familiar Conradian pattern of the discovery of a divided nature in circumstances of isolation and stress, opens the way to the main dramatic issue in *The Shadow Line*. Having obtained a terrifying glimpse of the dark powers within himself, the Captain struggles through the ensuing conflict between the normal and the perverse to an acceptance of the normal, of the sad wisdom of maturity formulated by Giles in his last statement: "Precious little rest in life for anybody" (XVII, 132). As almost always in Conrad, moreover, this drama of redemption proceeds from a fall conceived as an act of rebellion against tradition, the bond between living and dead maintained by the fellowship of the sea. In the nightmare of the calm with its assault upon the senses and the mind, the Captain recognizes his weakness before the terrors in himself and in the external world and learns the meaning of a personal bond by force of his dependence upon Ransome.

In great measure, too, the Captain's deliverance from evil depends upon his willingness to act, to take the deck of his ship with at least a pretense of the gestures of a commander, rather than to sink himself in contemplation of the perverse logic of affairs; and this assertion of the power to act is a human revolt against a world devoid of motion. So long as he remains below with Burns in the stillness of the cabin, the Captain absorbs the poison of the mate's sick fancies; and any hint of prolonged introspection summons Ransome to remind him to resume his watch above. On his return to shore he remembers the anguish of his becalmed state with so much dread that he launches at once into a bustle of activity. The importance attached to this antinomy of passivity and action in *The Shadow Line* calls attention once more to the persistence of this theme in Conrad's work. From an earlier attitude of reserve on this point Conrad reaches in time a stage where he becomes uneasy at the thought of a suspension of normal movement either through a paralysis of physical motion or through the silent brooding of the mind upon itself. This view finds expression in images of stone or metal, as in *Nostromo* and "The Planter," in descriptions of catalepsy, as in *The Secret Agent*, or of intense self-absorption, as at the opening of "The Secret Sharer." The sense of something deathlike or evil manifesting itself in an atmosphere of stillness or secrecy, like that in the silence of Hervey's house in "The Return" and in the choking air of Anthony's cabin in *Chance*, grows almost obsessive as Conrad matures in his art and proclaims, as in *Victory*, his distrust of doctrines of negation. The blade of his irony bites hard into modern creeds which savor of Oriental or occult philosophies of detachment; and although in a place or two in his essays Conrad mentions "the wisdom of the East" as important to a world which prefers act to meditation,[2] the East, when treated as a setting in his stories, usually appears dangerous to the energy and will of the white man. It is against the East that the Ulyssean Giles in *The Shadow Line* warns the Captain, who is drifting towards Jim's renunciation of effort and who later appreciates the warning in his desire to escape to sea from the pestilential Oriental town with its pagodas and temples crumbling in the light and heat. Conrad's mistrust of the East as a source of influences which enfeeble the will can be related to his fear of the void without creative light and of the mind's separation from the external

2. Conrad, III: *Notes on Life and Letters*, 88.

world from which it turns to shrink before the face of despair or at a vision of those depths that wrung from Kurtz his final cry, "the horror."

A horror of unrestrained emotions and of the loss of complete self-possession seems, in fact, to have been native to Conrad's temperament to judge by these words in *A Personal Record:*

> I will make bold to say that neither at sea nor ashore have I ever lost the sense of responsibility. There is more than one sort of intoxication. Even before the most seductive reveries I have remained mindful of that sobriety of interior life, that asceticism of sentiment, in which alone the naked form of truth, such as one conceives it, such as one feels it, can be rendered without shame. . . . I have tried to be a sober worker all my life—all my two lives. I did so from taste, no doubt, having an instinctive horror of losing my sense of full self-possession, but also from artistic conviction.
>
> (VI, 111–12)

Conrad's knowledge of "a mankind always so tragically eager for self-destruction,"[3] of the ways by which self-possession and humanity may be lost, and of the havoc to be wrought in the individual and in society by forces of unreason makes him one of the great interpreters of the irrational in modern British literature, perhaps the greatest before the Freudian era. In his novels and tales man's enemy lies concealed in the darkness within himself or just beyond the circle of his ordered world and ready to start into sudden anger like the death dwelling in Ransome's heart. The same malign powers that pluck down the would-be heroes—Jim,

3. Conrad, XIII: *The Secret Agent*, ix.

Gould, Lingard, and the rest—strive to penetrate the shell surrounding the created universe of *Typhoon* or *Victory* or to vent their wrath in the floods and explosions of the cataclysmic realm of Conrad's invention. In *The Shadow Line* the darkness closes upon the ship with the same promise of world-ruin that is written upon the sky in the final scenes of *Victory* where the lonely man and woman enter a struggle to survive. In this supreme hour of his initiation the Captain, once tempted like Heyst to drift on with the tides of circumstance, recognizes the need, exasperated by his helplessness, to perform the act which defends creation against chaos.

So somber a view of man's precarious state allows for little faith in human powers or in human survival without external safeguards, and for this reason the view of man as a limited being is central to the drama in the bulk of Conrad's fiction. It is a belief which inspires his subtlest ironies as well as the tragic outlines of so many of his tales. It is also at the root of his perception that harmony of mind and instinct is essential to the complete individual. That a bond between men or a tradition like that of the seafaring order should exist to prevent division or the evil which follows man's indulgence in folly or egotism is the conclusion toward which most of his writing points, but one of the strongest indications of his modernity is the fact that he asserts this need while doubting its fulfillment. His power to stimulate rather than to depress the reader springs, however, from a source untainted by despair. It derives ultimately from his fidelity to life and his resistance to death, these attitudes being no less essential to the allegorical pattern of his work than the myth of the Fall and nowhere better exemplified than in the theme of continuity at the heart of that fine record of human trial and endurance, *The Shadow Line*.

Bibliography » Index

BIBLIOGRAPHY

All references to Conrad's works, except for his dramatic version of *The Secret Agent*, are to the Kent Edition listed under the Conrad entry. Whenever the source was readily identifiable, volume and page numbers were inserted within parentheses in the text. Further identification is available by checking the number of the volume against the bibliographical entry for the Kent Edition.

Aubry, G. Jean-. *Joseph Conrad: Life and Letters*. Garden City, N. Y.: Doubleday, Page and Co., 1927. 2 vols.

———. *Vie de Conrad*. Paris: Librairie Gallimard, 1947.

Baillot, A. *Influence de la philosophie de Schopenhauer en France (1860–1900)*. Paris: J. Vrin, 1927.

Bancroft, William Wallace. *Joseph Conrad: His Philosophy of Life*. Boston: Stratford Co., 1933.

Bendz, Ernst. *Joseph Conrad: An Appreciation*. Gothenburg: N. J. Gumpert, 1923.

Bourget, Paul. "Gustave Flaubert," *Oeuvres complètes de Paul Bourget*. Paris: Librairie Plon, 1899. Vol. I: *Essais de psychologie contemporaine*, pp. 97–147.

Bibliography

Bradbrook, M. C. *Joseph Conrad: Poland's English Genius.* New York: Macmillan Co., 1941.

Conrad, Joseph. *Complete Works.* Garden City, N. Y.: Doubleday, Page and Co., 1926. 26 vols.

I *The Arrow of Gold*
II *Chance*
III *Notes on Life and Letters*
IV *The Mirror of the Sea*
V *The Inheritors*
VI *A Personal Record*
VII *Romance*
VIII *Tales of Unrest*
IX *Nostromo*
X *Within the Tides*
XI *Almayer's Folly*
XII *The Rescue*
XIII *The Secret Agent*
XIV *An Outcast of the Islands*
XV *Victory*
XVI *Youth: A Narrative, and Two Other Stories*
XVII *The Shadow Line*
XVIII *A Set of Six*
XIX *'Twixt Land and Sea*
XX *Typhoon and Other Stories*
XXI *Lord Jim*
XXII *Under Western Eyes*
XXIII *The Nigger of the Narcissus*
XXIV *The Rover*
XXV *Suspense*
XXVI *Tales of Hearsay*

———. *Letters from Joseph Conrad: 1895–1924.* Ed. Edward Garnett. Indianapolis: Bobbs-Merrill Co., 1928.

———. *Letters of Joseph Conrad to Marguerite Poradowska, 1890–1920.* Ed. John A. Gee and Paul J. Sturm. New Haven, Conn.: Yale University Press, 1940.

———. *Letters of Joseph Conrad to Richard Curle.* Ed. Richard Curle. New York: Crosby Gaige, 1928.

———. *The Secret Agent: A Drama in Three Acts.* London: T. Werner Laurie, 1923.

Crankshaw, Edward. *Joseph Conrad: Some Aspects of the Art of the Novel.* London: John Lane, 1936.

Curle, Richard. *Joseph Conrad: A Study*. New York: Doubleday, Page and Co., 1914.

Demarest, D. L. *L'Expression figurée et symbolique dans l'oeuvre de Gustave Flaubert.* Paris: Louis Conard, 1931.

Ferran, André. *L'Esthétique de Baudelaire.* Paris: Librairie Hachette, 1933.

Flaubert, Gustave. *The Temptation of St. Anthony*. Trans. Lafcadio Hearn. Garden City, N. Y.: Halcyon House, n. d.

Ford, Ford Madox. *Joseph Conrad: A Personal Remembrance.* London: Duckworth and Co., 1924.

———. *Memories and Impressions.* New York and London: Harper and Brothers, 1911.

Forster, E. M. "Joseph Conrad: A Note," *Abinger Harvest.* New York: Harcourt, Brace and Co., 1936. Pp. 136–41.

Gordan, John D. *Joseph Conrad: The Making of a Novelist.* Cambridge, Mass.: Harvard University Press, 1940.

Guerard, Albert J. *Joseph Conrad.* (Direction Series, No. 1.) New York: New Directions, 1947.

Hewitt, Douglas John. *Conrad: A Reassessment.* London: Bowes, 1952.

Huysmans, J.-K. *Against the Grain.* Trans. Havelock Ellis. New York: Modern Library, 1930.

Isherwood, Christopher. *The Condor and the Cows.* New York: Random House, 1949.

Kenner, Hugh. *The Poetry of Ezra Pound.* London: Faber and Faber, 1951.

Leavis, F. R. *The Great Tradition.* New York: G. W. Stewart, 1948.

Mégroz, R. L. *Joseph Conrad's Mind and Method.* London: Faber and Faber, 1931.

Morf, Gustav. *The Polish Heritage of Joseph Conrad.* London: Sampson Low, Marston and Co., n. d.

Praz, Mario. *The Romantic Agony.* London: Oxford University Press, 1933.

Retinger, J. H. *Conrad and His Contemporaries.* New York: Roy, 1943.

Thibaudet, Albert. *Gustave Flaubert, 1821–1880.* Paris: Plon, Nourrit, et Cie., 1922.

Tymms, Ralph. *Doubles in Literary Psychology.* Cambridge, England: Bowes and Bowes, 1949.

Wright, Walter F. *Romance and Tragedy in Joseph Conrad.* Lincoln, Nebr.: University of Nebraska Press, 1949.

Zabel, Morton D. (ed.). *The Portable Conrad.* New York: Viking Press, 1947.

INDEX

Index

Index